Endorsements for *Quest for Antarctica*

John Barell's book is a rich and ripping read that will not only captivate but also educate its audience. The book is a personal journey, guiding the reader through the life of the author and his Antarctic fascination. It explores how a young man developed an abiding interest that drew him ever southward to the Antarctic; this human story is both moving and insightful, coming as it does from the unique perspective of an educator. It also is a tall tale of human exploration of the continent itself, probing its geography and history, and providing a first person account of a remarkable journey in that most forbidding yet enticing land.

And finally, it is a slice of life in the Navy during an epoch era, touching on a diverse canvas of naval history and its central role in the U.S. involvement in the Antarctic. *Anybody who has ever been a parent will come away moved. Anybody who has been interested in Antarctica will come away with new perspectives on the continent they thought they understood.*

Dr. Susan Solomon, Antarctic scientist (NOAA), Nobel Peace Prize Winner (2007) as Co-Chair, Working Group One, IPCC, National Medal of Science winner (1999) and author of *The Coldest March—Scott's Fatal Antarctic Expedition*, 2001

I found *Quest for Antarctica—A Journey of Wonder and Discovery* fascinating because it reflects much of my own thinking based on experiences similar to—and often identical with—those that John Barell relates. Both of our lives were significantly influenced by trips to America's McMurdo Antarctic station that we made at the same time and at the same age. Admiral Byrd played a major role in both our destinies. Both of us are authors of books on Antarctica that feature disillusionment as a major theme. John's book is a memoir I might have written. It shows that encountering the Antarctic, reading histories of Antarctic exploration, and serving in the navy teach lessons for living that are transferable to other life situations. Through his own experiences, his failures as well as his successes, John stresses the importance of continually asking questions and highlights the need to be bold, courageous, and willing to test oneself. *Suffused with John's passion for the education and personal development of young people, the book will appeal especially to educators. Readers with military interests will be attracted by John's account of his time in the navy and his Antarctic trip, his meeting with Admiral Byrd, and his commentary on Byrd's expeditions.*

Eugene Rodgers, historian and author of *Beyond the Barrier—The Story of Byrd's First Antarctic Expedition*, 1990

Having "been there and done that" I can attest to Mr. Barell's accounts of the "Roaring 40s" and "Furious 50s" as the USS *Glacier* made her way south from Christchurch, New Zealand to the Antarctic ice pack.

Mr. Barell's quality narratives are a result of his profound examination of the historic record of Antarctica from undergraduate study at Harvard to professor emeritus status at Montclair State University and his personal contacts with Admiral Byrd as a young boy growing up in Mass.

His desire to experience the danger and sense of exploration of the early Antarctic explorers are juxtaposed with his personal "explorations" of life's mysterious paths, which results in a terrific and educational read.

Commander Don Epperson USNR (Ret) – Veteran of two Antarctic Cruises (Operation Deep Freeze) and Communications Officer, *USS Glacier*

Quest for Antarctica is a fascinating and candid account of Antarctic exploration, taking us aboard the USS Glacier as it pushes its way south during Operation Deep Freeze in 1963. While these waters have been the inspiration for hundreds of polar narratives, *this story takes unexpected routes: back in time to reconsider the polar expeditions of Admiral Byrd and their importance to a young man weathering his own psychological storms. In tracing this inward journey, Barell brings to life his struggle to reconcile the myth of Admiral Byrd with the flawed man who once ruled Little America.*

Dr. Michael Robinson, polar historian and author, *The Coldest Crucible— Arctic Exploration and American Culture,* **2006**

Other books by John Barell

Playgrounds of Our Minds (1980)

Opening the American Mind (1988)

Teaching for Thoughtfulness (1990, 95)

". . . Ever Wonder. . ?" (1992)

Developing More Curious Minds (2003)

Problem-Based Learning—An Inquiry Approach (2007)

Why are school buses always yellow? Teaching Inquiry PreK-5 (2007)

Short Stories:

"Twenty Below," 1955, *Boys' Life* and *Boys' Life Anthology*

Novels:

Surviving Erebus—An Antarctic Adventure onboard Her Majesty's Ships Erebus *and* Terror (2007)

Quest for Antarctica

A Journey of Wonder and Discovery

John F. Barell

iUniverse, Inc.
Bloomington

Quest for Antarctica
A Journey of Wonder and Discovery

Copyright © 2007, 2011 by John F. Barell

All rights reserved. No part of this book may be used or reproduced by any means, graphic, electronic, or mechanical, including photocopying, recording, taping or by any information storage retrieval system without the written permission of the publisher except in the case of brief quotations embodied in critical articles and reviews.

iUniverse books may be ordered through booksellers or by contacting:

iUniverse
1663 Liberty Drive
Bloomington, IN 47403
www.iuniverse.com
1-800-Authors (1-800-288-4677)

Because of the dynamic nature of the Internet, any web addresses or links contained in this book may have changed since publication and may no longer be valid. The views expressed in this work are solely those of the author and do not necessarily reflect the views of the publisher, and the publisher hereby disclaims any responsibility for them.

Any people depicted in stock imagery provided by Thinkstock are models, and such images are being used for illustrative purposes only.

Certain stock imagery © Thinkstock.

ISBN: 978-1-4620-2121-5 (sc)
ISBN: 978-1-4620-2122-2 (e)

Printed in the United States of America

iUniverse rev. date: 07/07/2011

For my grandparents,

Florence Wright Ferguson and
Llewellyn Ray Ferguson

And my parents,

Elizabeth Lockwood Ferguson Barell
and
Ralph James Barell

With loving thanks for setting and guiding me on this amazing journey of exploration and discovery.

Contents

List of Photos xi

Acknowledgements xiii

Introduction to ebook edition, 2011 xv

Preface xvii

Chapter 1.   Glacier Sails South 1

Chapter 2.   Calibrating Imagination 25

Chapter 3.   "Stately white caravels" from Little America 34

Chapter 4.   Through the pack—"Balls to the Wall!" 44

Chapter 5.   Sea Life—Adelies, Weddells and Killers 53

Chapter 6.   The Immensity! 62

Chapter 7.   "Don't try, Dammit! Do it!" 78

Chapter 8.   Bud Waite and the Truth 88

Chapter 9.   The uniqueness of snowflakes 97

Chapter 10. Vostok—near the Point of Inaccessibility 109

Chapter 11. Grains of Sand like the Gobi Desert 114

Part II: New Horizons

Chapter 12. Running aground 123

Chapter 13. Panama Dictator Torrijos 132

Part III: Beyond the Barrier

Chapter 14.   "Terrified of flying" 141

Chapter 15.   Remembering 22 November, 1963. 148

Chapter 16.   At last a reckoning 153

Chapter 17.   The Infinite Sandbox 157

Afterword—A View from the Conning Tower. 167

About the Author 183

List of Photos

1. Florence Wright and L. Ray Ferguson, 25th wedding anniversary, Atlantic City, 1936. 19
2. Ralph James Barell, 1931, upon graduation from Hibbing Junior College. 20
3. USS *Glacier* (AGB-4) in dry dock, Wellington, New Zealand, 1963. 21
4. Little America under construction, The Mess Hall, 1928 22
5. The radio towers communicating with KDKA and WGY. 22
6. Admiral Byrd's "Capital City, 1928 on the Ross Ice Barrier. 23
7. "You have the smile of a Hollywood actor." Admiral Richard E. Byrd and John F. Barell, 9 Brimmer Street, Boston, 1952. 23
8. Admiral Byrd photographed by the author. 24
9. Richard E. Byrd at Advance Base, 1934. "Grease the pan!" 43
10. Scanning icebergs for signs of Little America 52
11. Author offering nest-building stones to Adelie penguins 60
12. . . . with a playful Weddell seal 60
13. Emperors on full-dress parade inspection 61
14. Tent Island explorations 77
15. Pete Demas, Dr. Thomas Poulter and Bud Waite depart for third time for Advance Base, August, 1934 with temperatures at -75. 96
16. Winging past Erebus enroute Vostok 108

17. Royal Society Range where Frank Debenham, found "sand grains" similar to those of Gobi Desert. 119

18. The loneliness of long distance travelers 119

19. Elizabeth, Marcia, Ray, Anne and Wright Ferguson. 164

20. Elizabeth Lockwood Ferguson Barell with her first born. 165

21. Admiral Byrd on cover of scrapbook kept by one of his secretaries.. 166

Acknowledgements

My grandmother, Florence Wright Ferguson, suggested that I read a book by Admiral Richard E. Byrd about his expeditions to Antarctica and the establishment of his base camp, Little America. I read that book in seventh grade and so many, many more over the years as I discovered surprises about this continent.

Other members of my family have equally contributed to this amazing story that keeps enriching my life:

My grandfather, Llewellyn Ray Ferguson, scientist and creator of D-Zerta, who loved taking me on little jaunts around and about during which he would ask, "Johnny, did you ever wonder. . ?"

My father who, against my own will, deeply embedded messages of success with me like "There's no such word as CAN'T" and "Never give up."

My mother, Elizabeth Lockwood Ferguson Barell, who continues to discover fascinating information about Antarctica and Admiral Byrd. Without her loving support, manifested in so many different ways, this journey would never have developed as it has.

And there are others to thank:

My sister Robin Beck, an award winning journalist, for expert comments on later drafts, telling me "Here's where your story begins."

My sister Missy for being one of those who has continued to keep Byrd alive with found treasures from his Antarctic Expeditions.

Anne Ferguson Cooper, my aunt, for stories about her Dad's growing up in LeRoy, NY and for always challenging me with new and exciting ideas. And to Ken Cooper for being a wise counsel during some of the more difficult days at home and for teaching me how avoid getting sea-sick while serving in the Navy.

Marvin Stark, a shipmate and true friend from the days just after *Glacier* when we served in the Reserve Fleet as "weekend warriors." Marv slogged through much earlier drafts of this story and was always gracious with encouraging words.

Marytherese Croarkin, a friend and editor, who read a very early version and encouraged me to keep working on the ms.

Jan Williamson read a very early version of this journey and invited me to share portions with teachers in North Carolina, resulting in one of the most amazing and enriching workshops I've ever been privileged to participate in.

And there are others who, either by reading portions of this text or by the way they have responded in educational workshops to a much abbreviated version, have supported my sharing the story with a wider audience.

And, of course, enduring love and thanks to my wife and companion, Nancy, for often needed and incisive critique, for always being willing to read, listen and add her wisdom to these pages and, especially, for being a writer's best friend.

Introduction to ebook edition, 2011

Since first publishing *Quest for Antarctica* in 2007, I have come to see the whole journey, from meeting Admiral Byrd, sailing to Antarctica and becoming an educator working in our nation's schools as a life-changing experience. So often I find myself reflecting on various aspects of this adventure as having a profound impact on my life.

Standing atop two miles of polar ice cap at the Russian base Vostok always reminds me that Byrd called this a "limitless plateau" to explore and conquer.

Setting a goal to explore Antarctica "by the time I am fifty" became emblematic of what we do so often, set new Destinations that sustain us for a life time.

Having a hero like Admiral Richard E. Byrd was a galvanizing experience, because heroes do more than serve as models to imitate, or courses to follow. They mold character, even when, as is sometimes the case, our imaginations have fashioned an all-too-perfect image.

Imagination is what nurtured my sense of wonder about the mysteries that abound within this most intriguing continent on the planet. And fostering our own and our children's imaginations enhances our ability to conjure big dreams with unlimited possibilities.

Tennyson's Ulysses, en route home from Troy, said, "How dull it is to pause, to make an end, to rust unburnished, not to shine in use. . ."

So, Antarctica still calls out to me and everybody who loves adventure to imagine new horizons, set life-sustaining Destinations and experience the thrills of continual challenge and discovery.

John Barell
New York, NY
May, 2011

www.morecuriousminds.com
http://antarcticdreams.com
http://morecuriousminds.blogspot.com

jbarell@nyc.rr.com

Preface

Standing atop a wind swept polar plateau at the Russian base, Vostok, I was realizing a life-enhancing dream—to sail to Antarctica and explore its wild, expansive territories.

Here in the center of East Antarctica the polar ice cap is two miles thick with snow accumulated over millions upon millions of years and the winds whipping down from the South Pole chilled me through my Navy-issue foul weather gear. There were still hopes born years previous of succumbing to small white spots of frost bite on my ruddy cheeks and seeing my breath freeze before me as I spoke a word of greeting to my hosts. I adjusted my aviator shades to guard against the sun's intense glare off the sastrugi (frozen waves of ice) engulfing the base camp as far as I could see. The panoramic view was total whiteness save for the dark ice-drilling equipment towering over the lower red rectangular headquarters building and several swaying antennae.

Exploring Antarctic had been my project since the age of thirteen when my grandmother introduced me to America's foremost polar explorer, Rear Admiral Richard Evelyn Byrd. I became enamored of Admiral Byrd's four historic expeditions to his frontier town Little America established in 1928 on the Ross Ice Shelf near the Bay of Whales. Byrd's personal invitation to join his expeditions led to the US Navy, to McMurdo Sound and to Vostok in 1964.

Standing near the dark, hulking C-130 Hercules aircraft with its four prop engines roaring into the polar winds to guard against freezing in the sub-zero temperatures, I felt immense joy and satisfaction at reaching this high point on the continent. My goal had been to fly to the South Pole (some 900 miles further south) from McMurdo Station. There "the free world's most powerful icebreaker," my ship *USS Glacier*, continued to break a channel through the eight foot thick ice toward Hut Point where British explorer Captain Robert Falcon Scott had built his first base in 1901.

I had wanted to stand near where the Roald Amundsen first planted a ski pole with a Norwegian flag on 11 December, 1911 thus beating Captain Scott who, with his four companions, subsequently died en route home from the Pole to McMurdo in 1912 only eleven miles from a one ton depot of food supplies.

In 1964, during the heat of the cold war, no one knew of the immense fresh water mystery two miles below Vostok. Nor had the planet's coldest temperature of -128.6 F. yet been recorded here. We were in the early stages of discovering the paleo-meteorology of Antarctica and the entire planet from Vostok's ice-core drilling and my conversations with one Russian glaciologist revealed none of the terror many felt at confronting the Soviet Union with hundreds of nuclear weapons.

Several years beyond Vostok there were other high points in a life as an educator—climbing the Catskills in early June with New York City high school students and discovering snow buried deep within igneous rock outcroppings. And a few years later I was leaping off a fifty foot telephone pole into the cool New Jersey spring air to grasp a brass ring suspended as if from the cumulus clouds overhead. Down below me were young, eager teachers impatiently awaiting their turn to experience Project Adventure as a way of learning how to challenge their students to take the risk of thinking for themselves.

In reflecting on this life and gazing back toward my first fascinations with Byrd's Little America I realize that this camp of rugged, sometimes brawling but always curious explorers had become my own model for successful living, for being deeply inquisitive about our world, and for living within our democracy.

Little America had become my personal Philadelphia—the crucible wherein my imagination constructed the good society of men committed to science, inquiry and camaraderie.

Antarctica propelled my own wonderings about educating children, youth and adults. Along the way I made amazing discoveries about heroes who at the time seemed, like "gold, pure shining and unalloyed," as one of Scott's men (Cherry-Garrard) had written. I learned where the real heroes in our lives often dwell.

My own searchings for truths from Antarctica has led me to appreciate how we all set off toward our own south poles, traversing miles of rugged terrain believing our destinations are closer than they really are, that our paths are clear. But Antarctica fools you into thinking you are safe, that appearances are reality.

Antarctica is not what she seems.

Inevitably, we all stumble and muster all our strength to survive. In the end, we arise, re-set our sights on the horizons beyond which lay those unexplored territories that forever beckon and recede as we move forward.

And therein lies the excitement, the passion for life, setting our courses to sail over new landscapes, steering our ships toward those unknowns where we all make fascinating discoveries.

As Captain Robert Falcon Scott noted in 1903 while sledging off from McMurdo across the same barren polar plateau on which I was then standing, "What fascination lies in that word—Unknown."

Indeed.

John Barell
New York City
April, 2007
jbarell@nyc.rr.com

Chapter One
Glacier Sails South

"I relieve you, sir," I said saluting Lt. Tom Dryden and taking the binoculars of command on the bridge of *USS Glacier* one early morning in 1963. With that salute I assumed responsibility for handling the "the free world's most powerful icebreaker" as she sailed south' toward Antarctica on this bleak February morning. Steaming through the "Roaring Forties" en route to McMurdo Sound. I was fulfilling a dream of exploring the same polar landscapes as leaders like Sir James Clark Ross, Sir Ernst Shackleton, Captain Robert Falcon Scott, Roald Amundsen and Admiral Richard E. Byrd.

Far more than following their journeys of discovery, I was earning citizenship in a community of adventurers typified by Byrd's frontier town, Little America, built on the Ross Ice Shelf in 1928. What fascination there was in that outpost with its forty-two men, in their high-risk adventures and discoveries of mountain ranges and territories never seen by man. I never realized while navigating *Glacier* through uncharted waters that their experiences would become a guiding spirit, a metaphor, for my entire professional life as an educator.

Glacier was the largest ship in the US fleet designed to break through the thick ice surrounding and protecting the mysterious southern continent from too close observation. Antarctica's massively thick white glaciers guarded the tectonic secrets of her origin just as the surrounding pack ice sheltered her coastal bays and inlets from human intrusion.

Glacier was a marvel of gray physical prowess in the ice. Whereas the men of the heroic age of Antarctic exploration had braved these waters in wooden sailing vessel named *Erebus, Fram, Terra Nova* and *City of New York* my ship had a rakishly thick steel bow designed to ride up onto the ice, crush it and send cakes and flakes flying off to port and starboard. With no bilge keels she had a watermelon bottom designed to prance like a powerful stallion in fields of ice and to withstand the kinds of pressures that had strangled Shackleton's *Endurance* many years before.

The US Navy built *Glacier* to penetrate the pack ice girdling and enlarging the continent in winter by one-third its area, and then to create channels for cargo vessels of lesser strength and durability to sail through and re-supply our various bases. It was the pack ice that had threatened to keep the men of sail from filling in the blank spaces of nineteenth century maps. *Glacier* 's mission on this voyage *was* to breach this icy lock-up and make way for modern day explorers.

It was 1963 and the US Navy was in the heat of the cold war.

As I stood on the centerline of this massive ice penetrator with her 21,000 horses of power driving through the dark seas, I realized that this morning's watch would be different from any sea adventure I'd ever undertaken. The bridge was peopled with the normal complement of sailors acting as the nerve center of the ship, bosun mate, helmsman, talker to the engine room, messenger and, on this special occasion, for me, Commander Edward Grant, Commanding Officer, sitting in his black leather chair on the starboard wing.

I saluted Commander Grant and said, "I have the conn, Captain."

"Very well, " he replied in every officer's normal response to the presentation of information, vital or trivial.

This assumption of responsibility was a normal occurrence, but for me it was an experience of transcendent importance. For over a decade I had dreamt of conning a ship through the waters from New Zealand to the Ross Sea pack ice and thence down along the elusive often fog enshrouded coastlines of Antarctic. I was now just a quarter century beyond my birthing and looking out of the tall rectangular windows of the pilot house I saw the formidable adversary, waves tumultuous and towering right up to the level of the pilot house some fifty feet above our water line.

Chapter One: Glacier Sails South

We were not sailing a straight and true course line south on the 185 East Meridian. No, we were wallowing in the troughs of these huge gray-black-green waves that sent our ship as powerful as she was rolling thirty degrees and more from port to starboard, back and forth relentlessly.

Before assuming the morning watch on this cloudy, dreary gray day, I had gone aft to the fantail to steady myself by standing on the ship's centerline like a sumo wrestler—shifting my weight from one leg to the other to get the feel of the ship's response to these gargantuan waves surrounding me. Back here I could feel through my boots the rumble of the ten Fairbanks-Morse diesel-electric engines driving the huge deck high electric motors that powered our twin propellers through the dark waters. The closer you were to the waterline the more stable you were and I felt terrific, proud of my presence on board and relishing every trough and wave crest we encountered. Now, I was sailing where Ross, Amundsen, Scott, Shackleton and Byrd had ventured before me.

Back here on the fantail early that first morning I loved the steep roll of the ship because it reminded me of Byrd's voyages across these tumultuous seas in 1928 when he led his first expedition in a small three-masted sailing vessel, *The City of New York*. This much smaller ship had been my magic caravel escorting me lands away only a decade earlier and now I was rolling just as the sailors of that era had done only with much more power beneath my feet rumbling and churning ever southward.

I owned the seas, riding and rolling toward the pack ice with steep gray-black waves surging ever eastward. At last I was free of mindless school exercises where we had to memorize information and record it in a test booklet. This was life to be lived at its fullest, drunk to the lees and, like Tennyson's Ulysses, I realized

> *How dull it is to pause, to make an end,*
> *To rust unburnished, not to shine in use!*

I felt the power of these engines coursing through the soles of my boots and on up my legs to my gut where my recent breakfast was digesting itself. The engines' rumbling made me feel more excited than even the sexual fantasies I'd harbored as a seventh grader leering at women on the pages of *Esquire* magazine.

On that day in February I stayed in the pilot house holding on to the railing affixed to the forward bulkhead near the Captain's Chair where Commander Grant sat watching the rolling dark waves and swaying with the ship at every trough. *Glacier* had a draft of 28 feet beneath the water line, more than some today's ocean liners.

We were sailing through what explorers like Byrd had called "The Roaring Forties," where circumpolar currents rolled around the island continent of Antarctica unimpeded by any land formations. Over the course of millions of years, these currents had separated a once temperate continent from the landmasses comprising Gondwanaland, Australia, Africa and South America. Antarctica, now enshrouded in two-mile thick polar ice caps, had once been a warm weather landscape with strange and wondrous reptiles and dinosaurs fighting each other for survival. I wondered how this process worked, what could move a continent the size of Antarctica across the face of the planet?

"Now all hands remain clear of the weather decks," commanded the bosun mate over the ship's primary internal and external communications network, the 1MC. Bosun Peterson was a huge man, with forearms larger than my biceps, each with dark blue daggers and roses tattooed on them. Peterson was a gentle sailor whose bark if sufficiently aroused could send a lowly seaman apprentice cowering into a dark corner, but today, February 13th he was quietly assessing the status of bridge personnel under his control, the alertness of all telephone talkers, including the lookouts who were now stationed inside the pilot house because of the extreme weather we were encountering.

Glacier had been to Antarctica virtually every year since her commissioning in 1955. Among the geographical locations of historic importance that *Glacier* visited on this maiden voyage was the site of Admiral Richard E. Byrd's four bases set into the Ross Ice Shelf called Little America, a frontier community I imagined living in with the intrepid explorers of his expeditions.

During that maiden voyage *Glacier* served as Admiral Byrd's flagship on what was to be his last expedition to Antarctica, the beginning of what we now called Operation Deep Freeze. Byrd had stood in this pilothouse where I now peered through the windows at Nature's fury dead ahead.

Byrd was the reason I had joined the Navy in Harvard's NROTC program back in 1956, just a year before his death. He more than any American had pioneered the exploration of this southern continent with the first Little America buried in the Ross Ice Shelf, a glacier the size of France stretching from the Ross Sea to the South Pole.

"What's our heading, Mr. Barell?" asked the Captain.

"184," I replied.

"Let's try to keep on track, please," he said quietly as he peered forward, always on watch, always on the lookout like every good captain.

"Yes, sir," I replied. Most captains will ask politely, often saying "please" as they give an order. Few will be the barking kind who rudely yell their orders at you. Their "please" is as good as a "Do it now!"

Soon after assuming the watch on what our sailors called "the Mighty G," I began to feel something strange down in my stomach, a familiar feeling I'd known as a kid.

As puffed up as I was with the setting where Byrd had stood offering suggestions about transiting the pack ice—something he'd accomplished more than any other polar explorer in history—I began to feel the engines of my innards rumble like those beneath our waterline.

Gone were the exultations of power and responsibility flowing through my body.

I had eaten a wholesome sailor's sea breakfast thinking that because I'd been sailing for over three years, I'd be fine on the bridge. What I forgot was that I'd never encountered seas like these. The Atlantic and Pacific Oceans in their majesty had never been like the "Roaring Forties" in tumult and fury.

I was feeling the sickness of the sea, *le mal de mer*!

As part of the Harvard Naval Program (NROTC), I had sailed on destroyers and heavy cruisers during summer exercises preparing for any naval engagement with Soviet vessels or submarines. Then as an officer in the fleet after graduation I had served on an ammunition ship carrying atomic weapons all over the Pacific and subsequently on an oiler just last year.

I knew the queasy feeling deep down in my gut caused by rolling, pitching and yawing vessels. It was always embarrassing to be standing in front of old salts with red hash marks for years of service sewn onto their blue sleeves—men who'd already sailed over more salt water than I'd see during my entire stint in the Navy--and feel sea sick, to feel as if you were going to throw up in their faces at any minute.

Not the smartest thing to eat such a huge breakfast! My mother used to say "John, your eyes are bigger than your stomach! Be careful!" But I didn't always listen to her. In fact, at times I had little control over my impulses. "You surfeit yourself," she said forcing me to consult a dictionary one more time.

No ship handled like *Glacier* and I was unprepared for walking up hill to get from one side of the bridge to another on the green linoleum tiles laid over the deck plates. I was unprepared to see waves that appeared to be higher than our tallest masts and got nervous.

"What if we capsized?" I thought. Godalmighty! This could be the end before the dream was fulfilled.

I remembered all those academic concepts I'd memorized in Marine Engineering three years back at Harvard: Center of buoyancy or was it the center of gravity? We'd defined the term and done some calculations to find that point on a ship, usually somewhere down by the engine room and learned later from our instructor whether we had mastered the concept on the hour exam. Now, when it mattered a good deal more, I could hardly remember what I had almost mindlessly memorized.

I recalled with some sweat on my palms Admiral of the Third Fleet Bull Halsey's losing a ship (or two?) in a typhoon off Leyte Gulf in World War II. Somehow the ship got into the most dangerous quadrant, another concept we'd learned sitting at desks in school that was now very much on my mind. Which quadrant would suck you into the hurricane's vortex? Upper left, right?[1]

My stomach was gurgling and destabilizing my systems no matter where the center of buoyancy might have been. I visualized it down below somewhere in the engine room spaces hovering over the huge diesel engines Lt. Tomcavage, our engineering officer, had shown me. The rotors of the electric motors were taller than I was and Norm opened a little gate and said, "Here, go inside and poke around." Amazing how electricity drove our huge propellers through

---

[1] "In a nut-shell, the RIGHT SIDE of any tropical cyclone is referred to as the NON NAVICABLE SEMI-CIRCLE (by shipping / marine interests) or the "DIRTY SIDE" of the storm. For example, if a storm is moving North at 20-MPH and has 100-MPH winds, the right side of that storm will have 120-MPH winds!î (http://www.sky-chaser.com/schurr.htm, accessed March, 2007)

these raging waters. Here was atomic power without uranium 235, power derived from electrons moving through a magnetic field.

I remembered the same feeling deep in my stomach while driving with my grandfather up the Merritt Parkway from Hartsdale to his home in Stamford, Connecticut. We'd have to stop and allow me to get out onto the grass to lose my last meal. And after seeing a double feature at the White Plains movie theater, I would get screeching headaches so severe that after eating dinner (a huge mistake!), I'd get sick in the bathroom at 2 AM with my mother sitting on the edge of the tub telling me to stick my finger way down my throat.

"It'll make you feel better if you throw up, John," she said.

I didn't believe her then, but struggled with those two fingers making myself gag and, eventually, throw up.

I usually awoke the next morning ready to go to school. You couldn't miss school. No one said as much, but it was an expectation from both my mother and father.

Now, looking at the inclinometer on the bridge move from its center position of even keel way over to the left as we rolled another thirty-five degrees, I longed for anything that would make me feel better—like being down below in my rack snuggled beneath a blanket and not in charge of all ship's systems as we rolled south.

I wanted to be anyplace but where I was, standing before God and the Captain with a stomach as riled up as the putrid green-gray oceans, feeling as if I were naked in the cold.

"Maybe I should ask for a bunch of saltines?" No. For someone who idolized intrepid explorers most of whom survived being on the trail in flimsy orange or green tents at −50 degrees polar weather, my discomfort was absurd and ridiculous.

No, don't ask for anything.

I yearned for the situation *Glacier* had encountered on that Bellinghausen voyage of discovery in 1960—getting stuck for four days in the ice with little hope of freedom. Even though we had huge ballast tanks that could rock and roll the ship, they were pitifully inadequate to free her from the vice-like grip of the crushing pack ice. *Glacier* experienced the same crunch Shackleton's ship *Endurance* had suffered and sank from in November, 1915 in the Weddell Sea. I wanted that kind of frozen yet grisly stability just now, even though sailors onboard for that 1960 expedition became very angry about the possibility of "wintering over" for five months of darkness in the ice off some "god-forsaken coast line."

Get us the hell outta here! they said to one another. *We'll freeze our asses off.*

I continued to stare out the window and wished I had the freedom of the lone brown albatross winging its way effortlessly over the white crests of these towering spume spraying waves. No one would be out on deck this morning aiming to shoot this polar messenger out of the murky skies as Coleridge's crew once did during the voyage of the Ancient Mariner in these same waters.

My uncle, Ken Cooper, had served during World War II on an LCI, Landing Craft Infantry, as a gunner's mate third class. During the battle of Pelilu in October, 1944, General MacArthur's stepping stone to his invasion of the Philippines, Ken's ship carried men and materiel up onto the beach fending off Japanese shore gunners as they landed.

Years after his service while he was building up his business as the owner of radio stations in Bridgeport, CT (WICC), he counseled me on survival skills at sea.

"What you want to do, John," he said leaning toward me and looking me in the eye, "is to keep your eyes on the horizon. That will help you keep your balance." His ship had been 158 feet in length, flat bottomed, and probably bounced around far more than *Glacier* was doing now. I imagine some old salt had told a very young Ken Cooper this while he was manning his .20 or .40 millimeter canon sometime during that horrific invasion in September, 1944 that lasted two months with thousands of casualties..

I'd followed his advice all during midshipman and fleet cruises to WestPac. "Keep your eye on the horizon." He never spoke to me of his wartime experiences, as most veterans of that conflict do not. But he gave me life saving advice.

Here in the "Roaring Forties," however, I couldn't see the horizon obstructed as it was by gargantuan gray-black waves mounting up nearly as high as the ship's bridge and cresting in sea spume flung so ferociously at us.

There was, however, a slight feeling of reassurance in the way we responded to the waves. The weight and depth of our machinery below the waterline gave the ship a ponderous wallowing roll deep in the troughs of the sky obliterating walls of water.

Eventually, with the men on the bridge watching me—the helmsman, the engine order telegraph operator, the telephone talker, the junior officer of the deck, the bosun mate—and the Captain sitting right there in his leather chair—I had to walk over to a sea green shit can lashed to the bulkhead and puke up the remains of breakfast, and then walk at a 30 degree angle back to my position on the starboard side to regain control of the ship.

No one snickered, but I was deeply chagrined at my condition.

I may have laughed self-consciously about it slightly when leaving the shit can strategically placed directly beneath the ship's 1MC communications system. Here's where the bosun made announcements throughout the ship:

"Now, all hands remain clear of the weather decks. . .Now, all hands lash and stow gear. . . Now all hands turn to. Commence ship's work."

It was 0800 and I wondered what kind of work could anybody do this morning besides hold on? The sailors on the mess decks had to work to prevent hundreds of white ceramic coffee mugs from becoming low level, but lethal missiles flying through their air spaces. The wardroom table had its green felt cover replaced with a plywood fiddle board with cut outs for our dining plates.

"Don't worry, Mr. Barell," said Captain Grant as he leaned forward to look for traces of ice this far north, "We're fine." He re-assured me that sea sickness happens to all of us and that the ship was in good hands even if mine were glued to the railing, my knuckles were white and my ankles were getting as sore as when I was learning to ice skate years ago.

"Tell me how you came to be on board *Glacier*," he said in his soft yet firm commanding voice. A former pugilist in college and patrol officer along the US Mexican border, Captain Grant had "that lean, mean fighting machine" kind of body that the officers admired—slim, trim, flat stomach and strong arm muscles. His face was etched deeply with lines from years at sea and his sandy, diminishing hair bespoke of a youthful elegance and handsome demeanor Hollywood would have found most appealing.

While holding onto the bridge railing right in front of the window looking out onto *Glacier's* bow plunging into the huge seas sending rockets of gray-green water almost as high as the pilot house, I told Grant how this adventure of mine had begun.

"My grandmother suggested I read a book by Byrd called *Little America* and that was the beginning," I said. Florence Wright Ferguson had heard Byrd speak on Mary Margaret McBride's radio show one day in 1951. McBride was one of America's first radio talk show hosts, bringing in guests like Byrd, generals of the Army, US Senators, authors and other newsmakers, both men and women.

During the radio show, probably 30 minutes long, Byrd described his expeditions to her radio audience many of whom, like my grandmother probably remember his first broadcasts from Antarctica back in 1928. And knowing that I had to do what all seventh graders do, present a book report that usually concluded with these words: "I liked this book and recommend it to all my friends" my grandmother recommend I read a story of true adventure and daring.

"I became fascinated with the lives of forty-two men living in that frontier community, setting themselves off to the polar mountains and preparing to fly over the South Pole itself."

I told Grant about Byrd's flight in 1929 in the tri-motor aircraft, *Floyd Bennett* and his major discoveries of Marie Byrd Land to the east.

As I struggled to maintain my balance and remove my hands from the security railing as if to appear more in control of my body on this wildly tilting platform beneath me, I told him about wanting to be so cold on a New England winter afternoon that I'd get frostbitten in furious snowball fights with my friends. I wanted sub-freezing temperatures and biting winds whipping through our suburban neighborhood to raise tiny white spots on my red cheeks that could deaden patches of skin and leave me with small blemishes of honor. Not pimples—frostbite.

I hoped the air would be so frigid while trudging through two feet of newly fallen snow at home in Needham, MA that shouts of joy at slamming someone with a snowball would freeze in front of my chapped lips and fall into the snow flakes as visible words.

If I made the mistake of touching any exposed metal on our 12 cylinder Lincoln Zephyr with my bare fingers, the flesh would stick and I'd be in agony pulling them away. But I was often tempted to try it just for the polar sensation of tearing my fingerprints right off.

In the dead of winter with the sun setting at 5 pm, I would tunnel into steep blue-gray snow banks to create little hideaways where I could

Chapter One: Glacier Sails South   11

escape family and friends and just be alone with my books, candles and a thermometer.

These polar explorers became my heroes, men who would offer up their warm bodies to unfreeze flesh or pull you out of freezing waters of the Bay of Whales should you fall overboard during unloading operations. In my imagination on endless flights of fantasy, I followed them from Little America to the South Pole and off to Marie Byrd Land.

I emulated their routines—up early in the morning, take a weather observation using the cloud identifications my grandfather, Llewellyn Ray Ferguson, had taught me. Like Bud Haines of Byrd's First Expedition I kept records of cloud cover and rainfall in.

I also became a photographer like McKinley, snapping pictures not of vast unknown mountain ranges but of our house and my new very little sister, Robin, as she learned to walk and talk.

Since many polar explorers seemed to keep very extensive journals, I started writing about my own little journeys into the snow. In one of my earliest journals I wrote that "I hope to go to Antarctica by the time I am fifty."

Yes, I wanted to see the Great Ross Ice Barrier, as Byrd called it, and the Royal Society Mountains across from Scott's last hut on Cape Evans in McMurdo Sound and what I thought was the only active volcano in Antarctica, Mt. Erebus. And I wanted to experience and survive the cold. But more than scenery what I wanted was the sense of camaraderie that comes with being on an important mission of exploration and discovery, working on a team of dog sled drivers moving supplies south to the Queen Maud Mountains, wondering what we would find of geological importance in these guardians of the South Pole.

Little America was my vision for all America, a community of daring, curious and self-sacrificing citizens working toward a common goal. While in junior high school I focused my turbulent emotions during these years at the center of the magic triangle created by three seventy-foot radio towers beaming signals of scientific exploits around the world. I lived at 23 Webster Park in Needham (MA), but Little America had become my refuge from the boredom of school and the bedlam of my house.

As the seaman telephone talker repeated messages of "No contacts" from the radar room—meaning we had no icebergs on the scope only static from the waves-- I told Captain Grant about writing to many of the explorers and to Byrd himself.

"Yeah?" said Grant leaning forward to see the high white plumes of sea spray rocketing through our hawseholes forward. He relished this kind of seamanship just like my father loved being bounced around in a DC 3 over the Rockies.

"Yes, sir, and he responded to every one of the questions I asked him."

One day, after weeks and weeks of waiting for what I feared would never come, and my mother saying "Well, he's probably very busy, you know," there it was, a letter from "Byrd Polar Expeditions" to "Master John F. Barell." I read it with excitement, nervousness and deep appreciation for Byrd's responding point-by-point to each of my questions about his discoveries and about the possibility of discovering oil beneath the ice. "You are entirely right," he had said about such a possibility. "We found enough coal in the mountains near the South Pole to supply this nation for a long time. I am almost sure there is also oil at the bottom of the world."

Byrd told me why Antarctica was important:

> As you know, the world is in effect shrinking with an ever increasing acceleration. This is because of the ever better transportation and communication. Thus, areas once useless become useful. Therefore, Antarctica is getting closer and closer to us. And besides, it is an untouched reservoir of natural resources, which this country will need more and more as time goes on.

He wrote that there was an area as "big as the United States which has never been seen by man."

That thrilled me, this huge, white empty space on the charts that maybe I could help explore.

This letter, typed on heavy white bond paper in deep blue ink instantly became a treasure for a young explorer. I knew immediately that I would keep this for the rest of my life. It is only after years of being an educator that I realize how significant it was to receive a response from a world-famous explorer to your own questions. Here was a man who by 1935 had received no fewer than four ticker tape parades up Broadway for his accomplishments at the North and South Poles and he'd sat down and written to "Master John F. Barell." I was thrilled, amazed and almost shocked that he had written what my mother most recently called "this very personal letter."

Byrd even gave me his telephone number, CA 7-4334 and suggested I call him to borrow any *National Geographic* magazines I might be interested in. I already had a few of my own with stories from his early expeditions (1928-30 and 1933-35).

I couldn't wrench up the courage to do that, even though while sitting in Algebra I would rehearse a hundred phone calls to Byrd. What would I say? What could I ask him over the telephone? I was confused, yet eager to press on, to delve more deeply into his own adventures.

Then one day Rear Admiral of the United States Navy, veteran of four of his own polar expeditions, Richard E. Byrd called from Boston to invite me and my family to view a film of his Operation High Jump, the Navy's massive "assault" on the continent in 1946, using planes, aircraft carriers, cargo vessels, tractors and even a USN submarine, USS *Sennet*.

"You met Byrd?" Captain Grant asked looking over at me momentarily as he grabbed hold of the oak railing right in front of his Captain's chair.

"Yes sir," I said still holding on to my railing and trying to swallow often enough, and burp sufficiently to calm my angry stomach as we continued to roll so severely that a faded and chipped, white Navy-issue coffee mug somehow tore loose from its moorings, flew across the deck of the pilot house, slammed into the engine order telegraph and fell in one rugged, Navy-issue piece to the deck.

"He was most gracious with me, my mother and two little sisters," I said burping again. "He commented on the flights over the continent where they quite unexpectedly found ice free lakes in the middle of the continent."

'Imagine that, John!' Byrd had said to me as if I were a member of the expedition. He mentioned revisiting the site of his Little America home bases during the 1928 and 1934 expeditions and there establishing Little America V for the International Geophysical Year in 1955." I didn't mention that my little sister Robin, then fifteen months old crawled around during the film pulling on the electrical cord and untying the Admiral's shoe laces. Nor did I mention that when my mother took our picture, Admiral Byrd had said, "You have the smile of a Hollywood actor."

Grant was fascinated with the history of Byrd's expeditions and his chatter kept my mind working so it wouldn't overly focus upon the subterranean eruptions brewing down below in my stomach.

"He was on here, you know."

"Yes sir," I said. "I remember-- just before I started Harvard--reading about his last sailing on board this ship. It was her maiden voyage I believe." Then in the spring of my freshman year, 1957, he died having only recently received another special commendation for his years of service from the Secretary of the Navy. At that moment I did not know of the horrible conditions Byrd encountered while sailing on *Glacier*.

After visiting the little green shit can once again, I told Captain Grant about volunteering for duty on *Glacier*. During the previous year, 1962, with President Kennedy enlarging our naval fleet to prepare for a possible nuclear confrontation with the Soviet Union over intercontinental ballistic missiles in Cuba, my shipmates and I converted an old cargo ship into an oiler to service the Pacific fleet. When we were still in the Mobile shipyard, the President and Secretary of Defense ordered all US forces to stand ready for imminent attack, DEFCON ONE. We were on highest alert throughout the fleet because of the Soviet missiles pointed directly at Miami, Washington and New York City.

When my captain said he could help me serve on an icebreaker, I accepted his offer because I was still deeply intrigued by the south polar regions.

"That's the story," I said to Captain Grant who was getting ready to leave the bridge for his cabin just one deck below.

"Well, I think you'll find working on *Glacier* a bit different from those sailing ships of Byrd's."

"Yes, sir," I said.

It turned out to be very different in so many ways I couldn't imagine then.

I had told Grant most of the story, but there were parts that didn't seem relevant at the time of our being tossed around by Nature's high seas like a leaf in a turbulent wind.

I didn't tell him about my father's role in this whole saga, primarily because I hadn't had a lifetime to figure it all out.

Ralph James Barell was a hotel man, an accountant, who claimed that he was responsible for creating the first corporate computerized reservation system while I was in high school in 1954. This was a major feat, since they—the engineers—kept telling him "Ralph, this can't be done. You can't make the machine do that!" The "machine" was one of the first computers to be used in the world of business.

My father insisted that you could do anything you wanted to. "There's no such word as CAN'T!" he ranted. "God, How I hate that word! It ought to be banned from the English language. There's always a way," he would lecture me. "Never, ever give up!"

He was so proud of his leadership, his spirit of innovation and creativity with this system he called RESERVATRON. Sending a room reservation from New York City to Dallas in under 5 seconds was an amazing, practical and efficient goal for him. Using the telephone always seemed fast enough for me.

My father represented the quintessential American Can-Do spirit. He was born and raised in Hibbing, MN, later Bob Dylan's hometown, where they dug for iron ore in the Mesabi Range Mountains and fished for pike on nearby lakes. Ralph Barell deeply believed there's nothing we can't accomplish if we put our minds to it. He often quoted Thomas Edison saying that genius was "99 percent perspiration and 1 percent inspiration." Make your plan and work your plan, he'd say, and you'll achieve your goals. He believed his most important mission in life was "to produce... produce" for his company, for his industry. That word has lingered about in my mind as a command whenever I loaf or get lazy. The force of its message to get to work and leave something tangible for the day has been overwhelming.

His messages had become the sedimentary bedrock of my life.

Ralph J. Barell succeeded in pushing his engineers to the limits of their imagination and technical skills by creating this reservation system for Sheraton Hotels. I assumed it was the first in the land, something to be copied by all other hotel chains in the country. Maybe it served as a model for communications among corporations around the world.

What I might have told the Captain was that one of my prized garments of what the Navy called "foul weather gear" was a black and green sweater my father had given me back in seventh grade.

"Here, try this on," he said one Saturday. "I've been saving it for you. I used to wear it out on the lake while ice fishing." I wore it through many New

England winters feeling the warmth of the thick wool with a little hole down by the belt line. My father must have been even slimmer than I was at thirteen. I wished I had had that sweater with me on *Glacier*. Even now more than fifty years after the event, I wish I knew where it was. It was a testament of my father's commitment to my adventure, one I hardly recognized at the time.

The furious winds whipped our standing antennas back and forth and snuck through tiny cracks in our bulkhead doors on the bridge creating high pitched screeches like those of steel mill whistles. Every half hour the bosun repeated over the 1 MC a message that pierced the furiosity of the winds: "Now all hands stay clear of the weather decks. All hands remain below."

"Mark your head," I said to the helmsman as I rounded out my description of the past ten years for the Captain.

"Course, 185 degrees True, sir."

"Very well," I responded uttering the words one Captain had told me you always used to give you a few seconds to think about any potentially dangerous situation.

"Wait 'til we get into the pack," said Captain Grant. "It'll be easier then."

"Yes sir," I said picturing Byrd's ships silently sailing through open leads in the encircling pack ice.

"I'm going below for a spell," the Captain as he slid off his leather chair on the starboard wing of the bridge.

"And I hope we all live up to your expectations."

"Thank you sir," I said saluting him as he departed. You always rendered your respects to the Captain whenever he arrived and departed from the bridge.

"The Captain's left the bridge," Peterson reported for all to hear.

And we resumed our steaming south at the best speed we could make in these wallowing seas, about twelve knots or so.

My ankles ached, my stomach regurgitated itself every hour on the hour, but I was still in charge until noon, the longest watch of the day.

I wondered how long it would take to get out of the "Roaring Forties" and into "Furious Fifties." Just then I saw two bright white Antarctic terns flying in tandem over the crest of the nearest wave. They zoomed up like fighter pilots in military formation and then started their dive down into the next gray, spray-strewn trough where they wove intricate flight patterns in and around each other. In their tandem formation these terns reminded me of my mother and father and their very different roles in nurturing this adventure that began when I was just thirteen.

"I hope we live up to your expectations," the Captain had said.

My expectations at the time were to explore the encampments of Scott and Shackleton, to stand at the South Pole where Amundsen had beaten out Scott over fifty years ago, and to live like the men on Byrd's first Antarctic Expedition, working in teams to sledge across the ice into virgin territories and to help each other prevent frostbite.

But I had no idea that these journeys to the south polar continent would transform my entire life. Far more than the fulfillment of boyhood dreams to follow in Admiral Byrd's footsteps, these days aboard *Glacier* guided my challenging young people to seek their own south poles.

In reflecting on these polar and subsequent journeys I have learned that a life of probing, searching for answers can begin with investigating a mysterious, fascinating continent, one where snows, fog, blizzards, ice shelves, and pack ice hide its elusive coastlines and two mile thick polar plateaus have for eons obscured its submerged landscapes.

There are Antarcticas in every domain we study, in every walk of life, in every wonder of nature, in all aspects of human relationships, their mysteries beckoning, calling forth our curiosities.

In recalling the seasickness and the flights into the unknown, I have learned more about my parents and how they made this journey of exploration, learning and experimenting possible. I've learned more than I wanted to know about Byrd, the man with weaknesses, than I wanted to know.

More important than all these discoveries about heroes who pioneered the exploration of the white continent enshrouded in frozen mysteries, I now realize that the real heroes in our lives may dwell in the spaces of our lives where quiet sacrifice, suffering and deepest love prevail.

And beyond heroes I have come to understand the transcendent importance of Little America. Admiral Byrd's frontier outpost became for me a mythic community of rugged, curious men seeking high adventure within supportive structures designed to avoid the ever-present dangers lurking below the surface of seeming civility—a model of democracy.

Little America was my Athens, my Philadelphia.

Finally, at 1145 that dreary morning, with the lining of my stomach aching from trips to the shit can, my relief, Lt. Dick Rice, blissfully said, "I relieve you, sir." No words had ever sounded so welcome. I handed over the binoculars of command and lay below to a dark stateroom, a bunk with an aluminum guardrail to prevent my flopping on the rolling deck. With a warm navy blanket pulled up tightly under my chin, I wondered about the kind of pack ice pilot I would become and about those two Antarctic terns swooping above the waves circling each other furiously and elegantly.

1. Florence Wright and L. Ray Ferguson, 25th wedding anniversary, Atlantic City, 1936.

2. Ralph James Barell, 1931, upon graduation from Hibbing Junior College.

3. USS Glacier (AGB-4) in dry dock, Wellington, New Zealand, 1963.

4. *Little America under construction, The Mess Hall, 1928*

5. *The radio towers communicating with KDKA and WGY.*

6. Admiral Byrd's "Capital City," 1928 on the Ross Ice Barrier.

7. "You have the smile of a Hollywood actor." Admiral Richard E. Byrd and John F. Barell, 9 Brimmer Street, Boston, 1952.

8. *Admiral Byrd photographed by the author.*

Chapter Two
Calibrating Imagination

Plunging into the "Furious Fifties" we battled against the raging Antarctic Ocean sailing south to McMurdo Sound to join other members of our Naval Task Force. We were part of Navy's commitment to peace-time exploration and scientific research known as Operation Deep Freeze, a massive support mission that grew out of all of Byrd's previous expeditions to Antarctica.

But most Navy men at this time were serving on ships of war, battleships, cruisers, and destroyers preparing for what everyone feared, a nuclear encounter with the Soviet Union. We were two years beyond our new President, John F. Kennedy's, challenge to defend "freedom in its hour of maximum danger."

Few of us spoke about the imminent threat of attack, but each officer and crew member knew both countries had thousands of missiles with atomic war heads targeted at each other. We didn't mention the NIKE anti-missile defense systems ringing our major cities, perhaps because we hoped for dear life they would never be used.

My first ship, *USS Mauna Kea* was an ammunition ship that carried atomic bombs around the Pacific, transferring them from one military facility to another, into countries where they were strictly forbidden. The nuclear weapons rode across our steel decks on their little green dollies made by the company that had sold us the "Breakfast of Champions," Wheaties, and so many other fine cereals--General Mills.

Most men aboard *Glacier* had practiced the "duck and cover" routines in school to protect themselves against nuclear attack, an experience we only knew about from films of Hiroshima and Nagasaki.

During the Cuban Missile Crisis of the previous year Secretary of State Dean Rusk said we had come "eye-ball-to-eye-ball" with the Soviets over their land-based intercontinental missiles in Cuba. Through the wisdom of President Kennedy's naval embargo of all cargo ships entering Cuban waters, we made the other side blink. All of us had gone to DEFCON ONE, the maximum state or readiness for war, but the Soviets turned back and we avoided a nuclear holocaust.

We hardly ever spoke about this hour of maximum peril for millions of people, but everyone from Captain Grant down to the seaman apprentices on board knew we were in a war very different from World War II, one that might result in what one statesman called "mutually assured destruction (MAD)."

We didn't feel the terror implied in these pointed missiles, but we all knew they were out there and probably armed for launch with the push of a button.

During the heat of the cold war we were sailors off on a mission of peace where we might just encounter scientists from the Soviet Union on different vessels, whaling ships and perhaps their nuclear powered icebreaker, *V. I. Lenin*, the only icebreaker more powerful than *Glacier*. If and when we did encounter a Soviet vessel I was prepared to converse with them in Russian, having mastered enough of the spoken and written language at Harvard to read historical documents and converse at a basic level. But what I knew about the Soviets suggested that they would be secretive and elusive as befit their totalitarian dictatorship.

On my next watch now fully in command of my sea legs, *Glacier* took a sudden plunge into a rogue wave dead ahead as we steamed into the "Furious Fifties" on our third day from New Zealand. The black waves had been pounding us from the west on our starboard beam, but here was a behemoth wall of water dead ahead and without time to alter course, we plowed straight on into it once again sending huge plumes of white spray up as high as the bridge through the anchor hawse holes on either side of our bow. We looked like a haze gray dragon snorting the blue-green fire waters.

Pencils and a protractor sailed off the navigator's table on the port side and the ship's wheel took an awkward spin to port as the helmsman lost control momentarily. "Steady as she goes!" I ordered as the ship vibrated crazily sending reverberations through my legs.

"Secure all hatches," I told the bosun mate after Captain Grant called from his stateroom to ensure all was intact below. I was still holding on tightly to the bulkhead railing and I called the lookouts into the pilot house fearful that they were in more danger from such wayward waves slamming our one inch thick steel hull.

The ship's frames shuddered mightily from this head on wave and I remembered another dangerous encounter with the sea that sent disastrous vibrations through a different ship off the coast of Santa Catalina Island just a year earlier--

During a normal refueling at sea off the California coast, we were three ships steaming into the wind at dawn. The oiler I navigated was between an aircraft carrier to port and a destroyer to starboard with huge black hoses out to each ship. As the sun rose above the horizon everything was normal, steaming a course into the wind in order to refuel vital members of the Pacific Fleet.

All of a sudden our world turned brutally chaotic.

"RIGHT FULL RUDDER!" yelled Captain Norton, skipper of our refueling vessel.

"Right Full Rudder, aye aye, sir!" barked the helmsman.

Jesus! What's going on?

Pandemonium set upon us on the bridge.

I looked up from my navigator's desk to see the aircraft carrier on the port wing looming as large as New York City skyscraper.

"RIGHT HARD RUDDER!" Captain Norton was running from port to starboard, checking on our distances from both ships.

The Officer of the Deck came out of the radar room and tried to figure what had gone wrong.

"What's your course?"

"276," said the helmsman.

"Jesus! Come right to 284!"

Confusion erupted all over the pilot house.

I looked out the port hatchway on the bridge of the oiler and saw this huge gray mass bearing down on us, slowly reducing our distance from 120 feet to

90 to 60. A relentless gray superstructure towering one hundred feet above our little pilot house, like a high rise building on its side was drifting relentlessly down upon us. I saw the men on *KEARSARGE* who had shaved that morning, almost saw their names on their denim shirts in the pale morning light, at last cutting away from their stations to save their lives.

"Cut all fuel lines!" yelled the Captain. "Cease pumping immediately!"

"Collision! Collision! Sound the Collision Alarm!"

Mayhem reigned in a military space where deliberate calm should have prevailed. But now naval instincts, well drilled over decades in Captain Norton's case, came to the forefront. We were ships *in extremis*, that most feared encounter at sea dreaded by every sailor, when any maneuver by either one would lead to collision.

Men slashed away at the heavy black fuel hoses joining all three ships and quickly the hoses were dancing in mid air like serpentine snakes charmed out of a basket, spewing black oil all over the decks and into the pristine Pacific Ocean of an early dawn.

It was 0645 on the morning of refueling operations, a maneuver we had engaged in many times since rebuilding this ship during the Cuban Missile crisis.

"Steady as she goes!" The Captain tried desperately to save the ships and his career.

The Pacific was surging between our ships as if it were flood waters cascading down the mountain side from a broken dam. Now we could almost spit across the raging torrent of water and hit the abandoned decks on *Kearsarge*.

"Steady as she goes!" Another vain attempt to prevent the inevitable. We slammed into the starboard aircraft elevator of *Kearsarge* as the destroyer on our starboard side steamed away unharmed, fuming heavy black smoke from her stacks, but escaping.

There is nothing worse than the sound of two ships colliding, of gray metal grinding against gray metal, tearing themselves into hideous strips, ripping rivets asunder, gnashing steel plates into horribly sharp shapes, as if Neptune were drunkenly smashing the precise and sea worthy contours laid out in the shipyards so many years ago.

Fortunately, no one was seriously injured.

Unfortunately, there were casualties in character and reputation.

The Court of Inquiry convened on board our ship.

"There was a lot of confusion on the bridge," I testified to the Admiral, Captains, and Commanders sitting at the green wardroom table. I described all the orders I had heard, where the ships on either side were, what time we'd made rendezvous.

"How many degrees to port or starboard does the rudder move with one turn of the ship's wheel?" one captain asked me.

I sat there in total ignorance flashing back to navigation school in San Diego trying to read or hear a bit of information that would answer that question. I used all my memory strategies I'd learned in high school and perfected at Harvard, visualizing the wheel and rudder and their operations; conjuring up pages in my mind and trying to read them; searching for an acronym I might have created that would have that information—all to no avail. Learning in schools had to a large extent consisted in finding ways to stuff large chunks of information into memory for retrieval, but I'd never imagined a circumstance like this one. It never occurred in the "What if. . ?" games I'd played while standing watch on so many evenings as Officer of the Deck. I'd spent hours figuring out what to do if a Soviet submarine surfaced off the starboard bow in the dead of night and an equal number of hours in silent "What iffing" conjuring possible collision situations, but never one occurring during a refueling on a placid morning in the Pacific.

"I don't think we expect a navigator to know that," said another panel member relieving me of my anxiety over not knowing this piece of information. I'd never even considered it.

And where was the Officer of the Deck during the refueling? they wanted to know.

I had to admit that during the crisis I had not seen the Officer of the Deck. He had repaired to the Combat Information Center for a cigarette.

During refueling!

He was smoking during the one operation when no one, not even the cook down below making hamburgers for lunch was supposed to smoke.

The "smoking lamp" was always, always out during refueling operations!

The Officer of the Deck, responsible for the safety of the ship, reporting directly to the Captain, was smoking a cigarette with the men in the radar room!

The Junior Officer of the Deck did his best to describe how he unwittingly allowed the helmsman to deviate from the prescribed course. The helmsman started creeping left toward the aircraft carrier and it was the Old Man, Captain M.D. "Doc" Norton, who first noticed it standing on the port wing of the bridge about 120 feet away from this gray behemoth called *Kearsarge*.

I did not need a lawyer I was told, but both officers on watch and the Captain sat there were their counsel listening to everybody testify worrying about their career paths from then on.

Kearsarge sustained one million dollars in damages to the starboard aft aircraft elevator. Our ship, *USS Mattaponi* incurred less significant damage.

Captain Norton said afterwards that the Navy allowed him to stay in the service, because his experience would be needed "in time of war." Should President Kennedy's trumpet summon us as a nation to combat in what he called this "uncertain balance of terror," Captain Norton's years of command at sea would make a contribution. During our long "twilight struggle" with communism's imperialistic spread throughout Europe and the rest of the world, men of Norton's sea worthiness would be necessary for victory. Otherwise, the Navy would have given him an early discharge or shore duty immediately.

The Officer of the Deck and the Junior Officer of the Deck received various letters of reprimand and reproach for their dereliction of duty. They bore most of the responsibility, along with the Captain, who is always, always the ultimate authority and always responsible for everything that occurs on board a ship of the fleet.

And my punishment for being on the bridge, for having some responsibility for this whole operation was a poor fitness report.

"You can appeal this," the Captain said as he handed me my evaluation for the quarter that included the collision.

I scanned the categories and looked at the comments he had written. The only one I now recall was the category of "Imagination." What exactly that entailed I'm not sure now, but there's no doubt in my mind what "Doc" Norton checked off.

"Marginal."

I had a "marginal" imagination.

I couldn't believe it!

"Marginal imagination!" Good God! Just on the fringes of acceptable. *Lower than whale shit!* as my shipmates would say.

"You can certainly appeal this," he said casually realizing that his career had been dealt a severe blow.

I said and did nothing.

Nothing about being marginal. Nothing about the unfairness of the whole deal.

Why didn't I say anything? Make no comment? Argue his description of my navigational abilities? my accuracy in plotting courses?

"Marginal"

This word bites into me like a rattler wrapped around my neck shooting its venom into my body! I still can't believe nor accept it.

I did nothing.

I'm not sure I ever told my father about these events or, at least, my role in them. But that was the point, "Doc" Norton had assigned me a role to cover his own record. He suggested that I had been a poor navigator all along, when I never missed making a rendezvous on time, including that fateful one off the coast of Santa Barbara. This was rewriting history—something the Soviets had done since they seized power as Bolsheviks in 1917.

I had majored in Russian History at Harvard and found many cases of the Soviets rewriting textbooks to suit their own political agendas. Here was another case of looking back at the past and seeing what you wanted to see devoid of any evidence to support your conclusion. Totalitarian regimes in the Soviet Union, Nazi Germany and Communist China did it all the time—educating their young in a mythical vision of what they want their stories to be thereby eliminating all contradictory evidence.

Here was a kind of naval McCarthyism right on board my ship, a hunting for demons and scapegoats to cover up misdeeds. Only ten years earlier Senator Joe McCarthy from Wisconsin had riled this country into witch hunts for subversives in government by making wild accusations, carelessly labeling people as Communist with no substantiation whatsoever.

Marginal!

From the days of sitting in the closet at 23 Webster Park zooming off to Little America to a few years later steaming off the California coast I had, according to "Doc" Norton, plummeted in my imagination's capacity to think of new and different ways to fix our position, to solve navigational challenges.

I had brought the ship to her designated rendezvous using not only long range electronic navigational signals (LORAN), but had also fixed our position the evening before by shooting Aldebaran, Betelgeuse, Sirius, Polaris and Capella, shot them right out of the twilight sky with the sextant and brought these readings down to the Pacific chart into a neat little triangle that indicated our position at 2000 hours.

Not only had we used these two methods of reckoning, but our navigational team had also surveyed the contours of the ocean floor to find the hills and valleys that marked our position, thereby confirming the other two means of fixing ourselves on earth. (Charts of the ocean floor reflected the incipient science of oceanographic cartography in 1962.)

I had almost flunked out of Navigation at Harvard, because I couldn't calculate star positions flawlessly in the forty minutes of class time allotted. I had great difficulty doing fourth or fifth grade arithmetic quickly and accurately and, consequently, made careless errors that resulted in faulty position findings. As a result I had to sit in front of the Naval Unit Captain Spofford and explain myself. He said he'd try to keep me onboard and, thankfully, he succeeded.

Thereafter, I struggled to find those position indicators once the Navy took hold of my life. Buoys, red and green, cans, black, lighthouses that blinked white lights through the gray mists off Tokyo harbor, beacons flashing entrances to Pearl Harbor, stars and rolling contours of the ocean bottom where mountain ranges go as yet unseen.

"I would have screamed like a raped Indian," my former shipmate Bill Flannery said.

My grandfather had taught me the astronomical term for a highest point in the sky, "the zenith." From that I learned about a "nadir," the low point. And this was the "nadir" in so far as taking control of my own affairs.. "You can appeal this," the Captain had said, but that never was a viable option.

I could have marshaled all previous fitness reports written by Captain M.D. Norton and laid them out on the table or in a long memo to the Officer-in-Charge, Bureau of Naval Personnel.

I could have acquired expert testimony from shipmates.

But I did nothing. Why? I've asked myself this question for years and years.

It was not in my make-up to question authority and never has been.

In high school we read the *New York Times* daily and I tended to believe everything in the editorials by Arthur C. Krock, "Scottie" Reston, Tom Wicker and others.

Don't question authority. Follow orders. Stay in line. Don't rock the boat.

Glacier pounded through several more rogue waves and I regained my sense of the moment, leaving the oiler and the aircraft carrier tangled up in my grim past of a year ago.

Now I realize that the failure of doc Norton's other officers and his re-writing history ("marginal imagination") led to pressing the boundaries of my own thinking outward, beyond the conventional where we begin to make a difference.

Like Tennyson's Ulysses I began to see that

> "... *all experience is an arch wherethro'*
> *Gleams that untravell'd world, whose margin fades*
> *For ever and for ever when I move.*"

"How're we doing, Mr. Barell?" asked Captain Grant as he sidled into his black leather chair right in front of the best window in the pilot house.

"We're maintaining course and speed, Captain."

"Very well. Keep it so."

"Aye, aye, sir."

Chapter Three
"Stately white caravels" from Little America

Steaming southward I kept my eye out for the inevitable "ice blink," a brilliant white reflection on the undersides of the clouds just over the horizon of the immense field of pack ice somewhere ahead.

But before we met the pack, we'd encounter the icebergs. Byrd had called them

> *"mobile extensions of the Antarctic itself,*
> *stately white caravels afloat on a painted sea;*
> *a sky filling architecture schemed and wrought by Nature*
> *from the marble quarries of the Ice Age."* [2]

First observed by Captain Ross, this major quarry came to be known as the Ross Ice Shelf or the Ice Barrier. It was here that Amundsen decided to set down his camp for the dash to the pole, a decision that helped him arrive there safely ahead of Captain Scott in December, 1911.

I could hardly wait to get to the bridge to stand my watches as we sailed south on Longitude 179 E, Byrd's meridian of choice to enter the pack ice.

---

2   Richard E. Byrd 1935 *Discovery*, p. 35. New York: G. P. Putnam's Sons.

I wanted to be among the first to see these flat tabular bergs, looking so different from the Arctic iceberg that *Titanic* plowed into that evening in 1912 on her maiden voyage sending her to the bottom of the North Atlantic. Had *Glacier* rammed or sideswiped that particular high pinnacled looking berg, her one and five-eighths inch thick steel plates would have prevented any structural damage to the ship.

After exiting the "Furious Fifties" we sailed south into the "Screaming Sixties." Here is where Byrd encountered his first "caravels" in 1933 so I expected we'd find some soon.

While on my noon to four watch one day in late February, I was again chatting with Captain Grant who, as usual, was sitting in his black leather chair on the starboard wing of the bridge closely monitoring the calm seas and his ship's movements.

It was somewhat unusual for a newly reported officer to be sharing so much of his story with the Captain, but Grant was interested in Byrd and his doings.

"Tell me about Little America," he said on an afternoon with the sun beaming wide fans of dusky golden rays upon the dark seas.

Now able to stand on the pilot house decks without holding onto the railing for dear life, I stood between his chair and the helmsman always looking forward to be the best lookout on deck, but only barely as Doc Norton had once taught me.

With the black Navy Bausch & Lomb 7x50 binoculars around my neck, I recounted reading Byrd's account of his First Antarctic Expedition in *Little America* (1930) and *Discovery* (1935), about the second expedition. Little America was comprised of forty two men, scientists, dog drivers, sailors, weathermen, pilots, machinists, photographers, newspaper reporters and tailors all living within wooden huts buried within the Ross Ice Shelf for the duration of the expedition. They endured one dark winter of five months without the sun, an ordeal that could have driven some men crazy.

"*Glacier* was over at the Bay of Whales back on her maiden voyage," Grant said.

"Yes, sir," I replied thinking that was the case but not remembering exactly.

"What'd they do all that time back in the 20s?" Grant asked as we both watched snowy petrels dive and zoom aloft over the gray bow away from the sea spume sailing off the crests of the dark waves..

"The pilots worked on the first expedition to prepare for the polar flight in 1929. The aircraft, a Ford tri-motor craft was buried in the snow for protection during the winter. Dog sled drivers rebuilt snow sledges for journeys across the Ice Shelf to the Queen Maud Mountains, the same mountains Amundsen sledded through to get to the Pole in 1911. During the second expedition Byrd wintered in a hut all by himself 123 miles south of Little America."

"Why'd he do that?"

"He said he wanted to study the weather."

"But why alone?"

"He said that two or three men would get on each others' throats in such a small space." Byrd's called Advance Base was about 9 x 12, buried beneath the surface of what Byrd sometimes called the Ice Barrier.

I told Grant that Byrd almost died from carbon monoxide fumes and that he was rescued by members of his expedition, including a radio operator by the name of Bud Waite.

"He's been on this ship I think," said Grant moving around in his chair and hoisting is white coffee mug.

"Really!" I said in some disbelief. Imagine that! Amory H. "Bud" Waite being on *Glacier*. What a thrill it would be to talk to this old Antarctic explorer.

It wasn't until years beyond this adventure that I found out from one of the men on Byrd's first expedition why he needed to be all alone living in this 9 x 12 hut in 1934.

What I didn't tell Grant about were my fantasies of roaming through the tunnels connecting the various spaces to each other—the Mess Hall, the Administration Building and all the work spaces. While sitting in seventh grade algebra watching Mrs. Lorenson diagram the elusive "x," (and when I wasn't fascinated with her gently bouncing breasts) I was imaginatively prowling around the neatly carved out tunnels beneath the raging storms topside on the Great Ice Barrier during the winter. I would duck in here to watch the pilots plan out the polar flight, in there to listen to radio broadcasts from KDKA in Pittsburgh, all about President Hoover. . . auto production. . .and maybe the falling stock market. . .

Glacier's long passageways reminded me of these tunnels in their finely carved sides. Little America's tunnels were lined at the top with boxes of food, covered with tarpaulin and then steadily flowing snows drifted over them creating the neatest hiding places for a boy of fourteen, even if in his wild imagination.

The tunnels of Little America were my escape from the imaginary blizzards raging over head in Little America, from the boringness of seventh grade and from life at home too often characterized by parental arguments and a newborn baby's crying.

I got off watch that afternoon without spotting any ice, only the occasional albatross, that dark bird with a huge wing span shot by Coleridge's Ancient Mariner with dire consequences. There would be no target practice on Antarctic wildlife from our decks.

My duties on *Glacier* included supervision of radiomen, each of whom took a turn at the key hammering out messages from Grant to Task Force 43 commanders via Morse Code. I was always amazed at the speed of their delivery and ability to decode almost instantly the signals being sent to us. At first I was unable to distinguish any of the letters sent out from their swift hands but, eventually, I memorized the Code by imagining having to send out various distress messages all over the fleet.

When Byrd was at Advance Base, during the winter of 1934 he was so inexperienced with Code that it took him many, many minutes to get even the most rudimentary messages back to Little America. Later I learned that some observers thought it sheer folly to have ventured so far out into the wilderness of the darkest, coldest continent without even "a Boy Scout's" rudimentary survival skills. He had to ask Dr. Poulter, his second in command, to relay a message to the Waldorf Astoria in New York about the trick of preventing pancakes from sticking to the frying pan during the depths of the Depression.

"Grease the pan!" came the response from the chef on Park Avenue .

Like any division of men on a Navy ship, radiomen were a highly skilled group that performed their communications duties with amazing speed and efficiency. Standing in the middle of the Radio Room with its haze gray linoleum and racks of radios, amplifiers and other power equipment, I was always keenly aware of their professionalism. But one radioman, Burns, caught my eye the first time I walked into Radio Central. He sat at his station pounding out a message to Fleet Commanders in a denim shirt with the sleeves rolled up above his shoulders exposing his well-tanned biceps. On each was a dark tattoo. On one arm there was red heart with the word "Mother" scrolled across it. On the other arm was a dagger and the message, "Born to Lose."

Perhaps inspired by the 1962 Ray Charles recording with the same words, these words written in bold blue letters on his tanned flesh seemed like a depressing note for such a young man.

"Born to Lose," no hope, always at the short end of the stick!

What my father would have said if he'd ever seen Burns! "Born to Win!" young man. "Believe in yourself and you'll succeed!"

The next morning I was awakened down in officer's quarters at 0315 for the morning watch.

When I arrived in the pilot house at 0330 coffee cup in hand, I looked out at the placid dark blue-green sea and saw only water and sky.

> *"Alone, alone, all, all alone*
> *Alone on a wide, wide sea."* (Coleridge, "The Rime of the Ancient Mariner.")

It was now light out almost 24 hours a day, as we sailed south and experienced what every seventh grader learns about—how the 23.5 degree tilt of the earth in its revolutions about the sun cause the seasons. It is because of this tilt of the earth that it is cold and dark in winter and warm in summer in Needham, not, as some Harvard seniors thought, because earth is closer to or farther away from the sun. And it is because of this tilt that Little America succumbed to five months of total darkness beginning in March, and not in October as the editors at *Boys' Life* had thought. Without my permission they had made this editorial change in a short story, "Twenty Below," I had written in Claire Slattery's high school English class, a story that won first prize in 1955. I was outraged, wrote them a letter, but to no avail since the story was in print.[3]

---

3   Here's what the editors wrote "It's only March eleventh. *The sun won't set for more than nine months.*" [Their language in italics.] Here's what Byrd said in *Little America* (1930, p. 196): "We last saw the sun on April 17th, but its beauty remained behind. It's official departure was not set until the 19th, but the following days were cloudy and we saw no more of it." My original, with mark-ups by Claire Slattery, English teacher says, "It's only March eleventh and the sun won't set until April 18." So much for trusting your authors, for fact-checking.

We were now at about Latitude 65 degrees south; it was February and the depths of winter back in Needham. Here we were beginning to experience the sun's rolling around the horizon's 360 degrees and never setting. So at 0330 it was light out, but just barely.

"I relieve you, sir," I said to Lt. Dryden whose Lucky Strike cough always sounded so deep and menacing.

"Keep an eye out for flat tops," he said.

Dryden was a "mustang," meaning he'd been an enlisted man—an electrician—who'd advanced his way through chief petty and warrant officers to become an officer qualified to stand watches. Often called "LDOs," for Limited Duty Officer, we called them "Loud, Dumb and Obnoxious." Dryden was, however, special. Captain Grant had a lot of confidence in him when it came to maneuvering the ship in the ice. Dryden was so good that often, unbeknownst to the Captain, he stood watches in the ice for another officer who never felt confident driving through the pack.

Yes, indeed. The flat tops were bergs characteristic of southern waters, breaking off from the Ross Ice Shelf many miles to the south. This glacier, a pie-shaped mass of floating ice as large as France, grows from glacial streams off the polar plateau and stretches northward toward the Ross Sea where her one hundred foot cliffs present to the mariner that barrier to any sailings south. Her sheer white and blue sides seemed to Captain Ross like the white cliffs of Dover.

At 0600 came the report I'd been waiting for from the port lookout.

"Bergs off to port, sir."

I hastened out onto the port wing, raised my 7 x 50 US Navy Bausch & Lomb binoculars, well worn about the edges, perhaps even worn by Byrd himself several years ago.

There they were, hundreds of them appearing to be about five to seven miles distant--a fleet of caravels sitting silently on a dark sea, bathed in the pink tones of the morning sun as Coleridge noted:

> *"As idle as a painted ship,*
> *Upon a painted ocean."*

You could just make out their perpendicular sides, like the tunnels at Little America. But as we drew closer and closer you noticed that those steep sides looked as if they'd been sliced from their birthing glacier at many different angles.

"Ask Radar to plot our CPA," I told the telephone talker.

We would pass within a few thousand yards and I needed to tell Captain Grant of the sighting and our Closest Point of Approach (CPA), another lesson learned from Doc Norton who always wanted to know, in addition to what you saw, its CPA and your recommended course of action. What do you suggest we do about this contact? If there's a problem, I want to know what you think we should do to solve it. Don't leave all the thinking up to the Captain; be pro-active, take a stand, be in the game.

In the case of the icebergs, stand in awe and wonder at Nature's handiwork.

"Your first, Mr. Barell?" Captain Grant asked

"Yes, sir," I said smartly putting my glasses down and looking dead ahead so as not to appear too enthralled by seeing live and in color what I'd studied for years in *National Geographic* black and white, and sometimes light blue, photos.

When we reached our CPA with the nearest berg, it was at the end of my morning watch, at 0745. After Lt. Dick Rice relieved me I hung around with a secret little wish.

I kept my glasses glued to all of the tabular bergs within close proximity and even some of those far off searching for a blemish in the chalky blue-white sides. I wanted to find that sedimentary layer of darkness twenty, thirty, forty or more feet below the surface that would indicate that there had been human habitation at one time—evidence that Little America still existed frozen in ice, in time. My binoculars searched from one caravel to another seeking out that line of dirt, mud, trash or grease left by the indefatigable inhabitants of that frontier outpost in 1928, 1933, 1939, 1946 or even 1956.

I was scanning the now white-pink behemoths sailing on a ink-blue ocean for the remains of a hut, perhaps the Radio Shack where Bud Waite tapped out his signals to a Depression-weary United States of 1934. How did the explorers live through that terrible time when I thought nearly everybody was out of work? Maybe some sailed south to avoid the breadlines.

Maybe I'd see the front axel of one of the Citroen tractors that caused so much trouble on their rescue mission to Advance Base. Where were these abandoned machines and how had they weathered the many winters since 1935?

Perhaps I'd find a rectangular hole, crushed under the weight of the snows above, representing the remains of the tunnel between Dog Heim and the Mess Decks, or just outside Paul Siple's biological laboratory where he skinned the penguins. What was Dr. Siple up to now?

As we got closer I leaned into the chilly air, pressing the binoculars closer into my face as if looking harder would make fantasy become reality. I knew that now, some thirty years after Byrd left Little America in 1935 that his outpost on the Bay of Whales had been buried deeply, but in December of 1955 after flying off *Glacier's* helicopter pad, Admiral Byrd touched down at the site of Little Americas I and II and stood next to the top of the two steel radio towers, each 70 feet tall in 1928. Only 8 years ago Byrd and Siple, the Eagle Scout he brought with him on each previous expedition, could place his hand almost atop that 70 foot tower as about 10 feet were still exposed.

"It's great to get back here, " he wrote in the August 1956 issue of *National Geographic*, "with about 10 buildings of my first two camps right under my feet. They're likely to be there for a long time to come, locked away tighter than a mummy in a pyramid, but their content still well preserved and available if needed. . ."

I might find some remnant of those buildings if I looked hard enough. Would the food left deep down still be edible? Could you still eat the eggs, make the coffee found in tin cans? Byrd always claimed that such was the case.

Nothing but sheer whiteness of the flat tops and the gray, blue, dark green at the water line of the sides of these stately caravels.

I so wanted to find evidence of that community of daring adventurers, a community that always seemed to me to represent the best of America herself. For brief moments many years ago there were men struggling for survival, planning to adventure beyond the horizon to make major discoveries of mountain ranges, glaciers and fossils of a very remote and warm, watery past. There was Little America, the essence of living in close harmony, creating, working and playing by their own rules, making decisions in the best interests of a major goal—exploration. Here was America in the frozen wastelands of Antarctica—forty-two young, adventurous, daring, brash, bold men, full of camaraderie, yet extremely vulnerable to dangers lurking in the nearest crevasse. A widening crevasse had threatened my fictitious expedition in "Twenty Below" causing men to move their camp site onto higher, safer surfaces on the Ross Ice Shelf.[4]

Little America was all of America in microcosm—full of men with superior qualifications, full of deep curiosities about the unexplored territories they were inhabiting, full of men with the CAN DO spirit that says nothing's impossible. We can make that engine work, fly that airplane, get to that mountain range given enough time, energy and passion for our work.

Nothing's impossible for him with a dream, passion and a commitment to succeed. *"There's no such word as CAN'T."*

And how would the *Glacier* officers and crew stack up against Byrd's men? Were they men of bold stripe and daring also? I would have to wait and see.

"See anything, Mr. Barell?" asked Captain Grant.

"All that's fascinating," I said leaning up against the port wing bulkhead. *Glacier* was steaming easily through the dark waters with all the stately white caravels bathed in deep pink from the setting sun's shining through the earth's pure, unsullied atmosphere.

I lay below hoping that Little America was still intact, buried somewhere south under millions of tons of compacted ice. Maybe the tips of those radio towers would be visible above the surface of the Great Ross Ice Barrier. I wanted and needed Little America when I was thirteen and now when I was nearing twenty-five.

Little America was my vision of the future.

Little America was one of the first geographical locations I penned onto the chart of Antarctica I drew, with my father's help, back in eighth grade. I'd taken it in to 9 Brimmer Street, Boston, to show Admiral Byrd. He looked at it admiringly, took out a pen from his khaki summer jacket bedecked with campaign ribbons and signed it, "Good work and good luck, Richard E. Byrd." The same signature I'd seen on his first letter.

Little America was a hope for all America.

---

4   John Barell May, 1955 "Twenty Below," *Boys Life Magazine*. Anthologized in *Boys' Life Treasury—Selected by the Editors of Boys' Life*, 1958. New York: Simon and Schuster, p. 213.

9. Richard E. Byrd at Advance Base, 1934. *"Grease the pan!"*

Chapter Four
Through the pack—
"Balls to the Wall!"

The continents of earth appear fixed for all eternity, rock solidly embedded in the earth's crust with clearly delineated boundaries that carve out bays, peninsulas and beaches of the world's oceans and seas.

But each continent is part of a plate that forms the outer most shell of earth's crust. Over millions and millions of years these plates have moved across the face of the earth. Geologists think that convection currents (much like you'd find in a pot of boiling water) generated by heat from the earth's core move the continental and ocean plates on earth's surface at the glacial speed of two centimeters per year.

Today's configurations are, therefore, very different from their positions hundreds of millions of years ago. At that time north America and Europe were conjoined with no Atlantic Ocean between them; Alaska was an island drifting northward, California was out in what we now call the Pacific Ocean and sandstones and lime stones with marine fossils were forming in what would become the Grand Canyon.

Antarctica is different. It rides atop its own plate and it expands and contracts annually. She does so by creating pack ice every March extending her territoriality by one third the total land mass. Ice forming in the Ross and Weddell Seas and in the coastal waters in between forms an impenetrable barrier during the winter time extending her coastlines northward by hundreds of miles. Pack ice can be ten feet or more thick and for many mariners of the heroic age of exploration, this barrier represented their most severe challenge.

Sir James Clark Ross encountered the pack ice near where *Glacier* was now steaming, Lat. 75 South And Longitude 179 East . Ross had been commissioned by Her Majesty Queen Victoria to find the South Magnetic Pole and he had to decide whether to plunge his two small wooden sailing bomb boats *Erebus* and *Terror* into this sea ice. Officers advised not going in because if the north winds continued to prevail it would be devilishly difficult to tack back out toward civilization. These ships were 106 and 102 feet in length, respectively with 29 foot beams. They were tri-masted barque-rigged vessels with square sails built to hurl cannon balls (mortars) at an enemy from fairly close range. By comparison *Glacier* is 325 feet in length and the new *Queen Mary 2* tops out at over 1100 feet from stem to stern (with the Empire State Building from street to top is 1250, not including the lightning rod).

After some consideration Captain Ross ordered both ships south through the pack ice on 3 January 1841.

Later Roald Amundsen wrote of this daring feat:

> *Few people of the present day are capable of rightly appreciating this heroic deed, this brilliant proof of human courage and energy. With two ponderous craft—regular 'tubs' according to our ideas—these men sailed right into the heart of the pack, which all previous explorers had regarded as certain death.*[5]

In taking this supreme risk Ross and Terror captain Crozier discovered the whole continent that lay to the south and helped delineate the coastline of what was then "Terra Incognita."

Now *Glacier* drove on through the ice with 21,000 horsepower at her command springing to life as soon as she entered the ice, a thoroughbred prancing her way proudly through the engirdling ice barrier.

---

5   Roald Amundsen, 2001 (originally in two volumes, 1913) *The South Pole: An Account of the Norwegian Antarctic Expedition in the Fram, 1910-1912* New York: NYU Press, p. 12.

The ice we encountered in November spread out before us with only a few dark lines of open water jagged here and there on a white canvas like an abstract impressionist painting by Franz Klein. We bulldozed our way through fields of ice where in some places relentless pressure had created miniature castles of blue-white fantasy that sailors of Scott's era called "hummocks." We followed leads where we could and ran head long onto the floe sending conic sprays up over the gunwales on the foredeck catching the amateur photographers unawares.

Byrd and Scott had their masthead lookouts and so did we, only ours were officers and they drove the ship from high atop the mast, some 100 feet above the water. Here in that black box affixed to the mast that we called "'Loft Conn" you could steer and drive the ship using a magic box with two throttles on either side, one for the port and one for the starboard screw. The view from seven rectangular windows was commanding, stretching out toward the horizon some ten miles or so. There was room for an officer of the deck and his junior officer.

"Any leads?" Captain Grant would inquire from down in the pilot house and you had better know where there was a hint of open water. Besides the two engine throttles, there was a rudder command module, and a 21MC communications box that allowed you to speak with the ship's vital nerve centers: radio central, engine room, combat information center (CIC, where all the radars were located), and, of course, the bridge.

A very commanding position indeed.

Mark Twain once observed that there was no one in more total control of his own movements than a ship's pilot. When he navigated down the Mississippi in 1853 as a young man of twenty-three or so with full pilot's credentials, he noted:

> ...a pilot, in those days, was the only unfettered and entirely independent human being that lived [on] the earth. In truth, every man and woman and child has a master, and worries and frets in servitude; but in the day I write of, the Mississippi pilot had none.[6]

---

6   Mark Twain, 1962 *Life on the Mississippi*, World's Classics p. 96-97.

Chapter Four: Through the pack—"Balls to the Wall!"

I knew that I did not have the unfettered control in the conning tower of *Glacier*, but at least I reckoned that I could make propulsion and steering decisions that, within reason, would stand the test of scrutiny and not be challenged to any great extent. I had learned this from Captain Grant who expected that you would drive *Glacier* through the ice with authority and confidence. Grant expected you to take chances, to see beyond the immediate lines of ice off toward the horizon where there might be open water.

Be a risk taker within reason. Don't get too mired in one small patch of open water, but keep a weather eye on the entire field of play sweeping the horizon regularly to gather in as much information as possible. Captains wanted you to be alert, to think ahead, beyond the ship's prow to what lay between you and beyond the horizon. Be a big thinker, imagine the possible.

Grant was often in Loft Conn demonstrating how to maneuver in the ice, showing me and other officers how to charge, back down and charge again. He wasn't afraid to learn on the job and show his men how you figure out what a ship can do. He needed to learn for himself and he did so alongside officers who had learned some lessons maneuvering in the ice and from previous commanders. After all, conning this ship through the ice was like no other sea duty in the world.

"C'mon, Barell, this isn't some goddamned Wellington virgin you got here! Drive her, boy!" he commanded in his pugilistic voice over the 21MC (the inter compartmental communications system). No reminiscing about Byrd now, he was saying, get this girl going good.

I stood there, throttles in hand trying to learn the new craft of driving using the two throttles on the starboard side of the conning tower.

"Goose her good and let's get through this goddamned stuff, o.k.?" Stand on your own two feet, Grant said, be your own man up there. Take charge and show everybody you know how to drive. No weaseling off to the Army because you hated Harvard as I had contemplated a few years back. Now you've got the world by the gonads. No place to be "marginal."

"Balls to the wall!" Tom Dryden used to say about thrusting forward through the ice. Charge! Full speed ahead!

No pussyfooting around. Just take some risks and *do it!* That's how you learn, boy! Get in there and mess around! Sure, you're going to get into tough situations and make many mistakes, but that's what learning is all about. Look for opportunities to experiment, fail and learn from those misjudgments. That's all they are, miscalculations, stepping stones to knowledge and wisdom.

How far were we now from Mae Millikin's memory machines in tenth grade World History where you memorized your way from the Renaissance through European Communism after World War II! This was the proving ground, the test track that no 45 minute class in icebreaker driving could prepare you for at Harvard. This was "school of the ship" at its most rigorous. This was what educators now call "authentic problem solving" at its best—figuring things out in the "real world," not engaging in abstract, remote and meaningless text book lessons with answers in the teacher's edition.

Conning the ship was like living in Little America—plotting and planning how to sail beyond the horizon into lands never before seen. Keep the possibilities alive.

"Keep your eye on the horizon." Keep your attention on the possibilities of leads far out ahead and don't let the immediate grinding of pack ice down below over come your thinking ahead. "Make your plan and work your plan," my father had said.

Up in Loft Conn backing down or thrusting forward I felt streams of adrenaline and excitement racing through my body. All that power at my finger tips with just a turn of the throttle. Just like blazing down Great Plain Avenue in Needham at 2 a.m., on that imaginary black motorcycle of my youth, left hand around her bare waist, the right hand on the power throttle. Zoooming. . .pulsating. . .throbbing. . .all over town. . .hands at the ready. . .

"Balls to the wall, mate!" and send topsy turvy the huge chunks of blue sea ice with their dark brown algae frozen to the undersides.

An ultimate moment, being in command driving through massive slabs of ice.

At last I was in charge, just like Mark Twain.

But not completely. A year later, Captain Grant had been replaced by Captain V. J. Vaughan and we were again steaming through the pack ice.

"Who's driving up there now?" Captain Vaughan always wanted to know from down below. Vaughan never seemed to read the watch list and leaned over from his Captain's chair to press the lever on the 21MC to keep us on edge.

You got to watch those screws, goddamnit! I'm not going to take any unnecessary trips up to those Wellington dry docks so all you guys can screw around with your girlfriends!

This was a real change of command!

With Captain Grant we made two voyages to New Zealand to replace our battered and broken screws, and some cynical observers thought these were liberty voyages pure and simple. We needed our women more than the scientists at McMurdo needed the supply ships steaming in behind us.

Gung ho, gonads! Full steam ahead!

But Vaughan was determined to prevent that.

Every commanding officer is like a new teacher in the classroom, each having his or her own priorities and ways of doing things. You always walk a little tentatively about the ship with a new skipper onboard, wondering just how he will behave. What are his expectations? What does he want done that the other fellow let slide? How will he command?

Vaughan was indeed different. He was a submariner and spoke often about "losing the bubble," losing control of a situation, letting it get away from you, as if we were all in a submerged submarine tilting too far from a level attitude.

Don't lose your bubble, Barell! He commanded.

Indeed. Don't take your eye off the bubble. Be in control. Don't be like that junior officer on the AO-41 took his eye off the compass repeater. Keep your focus at all times!

Vaughan went shopping at the naval air station near Boston and got himself and the Executive Officer brilliant orange hunting hats made out of the same material Byrd had used to make trail flags to mark the passage through the Valley of Crevasses south of Little America toward Advance Base. Vaughan wanted everyone to notice him standing out on the wing of the bridge so there would be no mistaking who was in charge.

Again and again and again he barked orders from the flying wing of the bridge without ever venturing up the ladder to the conning station.

"Who's driving up there now?" he would ask incessantly from the bridge over the 21 MC. "Who's driving?" as if the answer would give him confidence in our maneuvering through the ice.

So when Vaughan said he was coming up to Loft Conn one brilliantly sunny morning in the middle of the pack ice sparkling with a few black leads and a few lazy Weddell seals lolling around in their tons of blubber, I wondered what I had done wrong. I always harbored this rather deep apprehension about authority and felt like the kid being called down to the principal's office.

So Vaughan was coming up to inspect, to take control, to continue in the tradition of Captain Sir James Clark Ross, the tradition of daring leadership.

Vaughan climbed the thirty-five steps within the mast up to the conning tower as the ship ground through the hummocks of ice.

"So this is where you guys hang out," he said.

"Yes, sir."

He took everything in as I expected, noting our course, speed our projected destination toward the horizon and our wake. After a few minutes of small talk, he took over the command controls and I stood aside to watch and learn.

Here was my first lesson with the new teacher. He would be different from Grant, but I would see how a submariner slams into the ice, leaving pack ice to spray off the bows and create a new pathway through the ice. Submariners might love to dive down into the deep, escaping the threat of enemy intrusion on the surface, running silently down in the deep beneath the storms of the day.

Run silent, run deep.

Being in a submarine would be just like walking alone in the tunnels of Little America, safe and secure from turmoil that raged above you, your bubble level for cruising.

Bill Flannery was one of my officer shipmates on *Mauna Kea*. He was a submariner who came up through the ranks as a quartermaster and who taught me how submariners work in the "maneuvering room," adjusting ship's attitude under water. Maybe the new skipper would be like Bosn Flannery.

Vaughan started tentatively with the throttles, pushing the port ahead a little, adjusting the rudder to set a slightly different course, then evening the throttles as the ship responded to his gentle maneuvering. Here was Vaughan increasing speed a little bit on the surface. I wondered if he wanted to submerge the whole ship and just sail beneath the pack as the nuclear submarine *Nautilus* had done beneath the North Pole.

"O.K. Mr. Barell," he said after a few short minutes at the throttles. He descended back down to the bridge and I was left more than slightly surprised at his short stint as commanding officer at the throttles, where the officers spoke of driving hard, "Let her rip, Jackson!" as Norm Tomcavage said to me on many occasions.

So that was it! He had barely toyed with the throttles; there was little of the love of experimentation that most naval officers experience when they first get to try maneuvering in open water. They take their ships out and mess around with everything, testing the turning circles, seeing how they propel forward through the waves and how much time it takes to decelerate to a full stop, back her down and see how long before she gathers sternway. That's what adventurous captains do! Just like testing out a new car.

But here was Vaughan, so different from Grant who reveled in treating *Glacier* like a new conquest abroad, seeing just how far she would go. Vaughan tried it out for five minutes and then retired to his chair down below on the starboard side of the bridge.

Maybe because he couldn't flood the ballast tanks and sink us beneath the pack like those nuclear boats up at the North Pole, he didn't want to mess around. Maybe he was apprehensive about losing his own bubble? his own guiding markers through the ice? Perhaps he had no mind to wonder about all the possibilities of propulsion way up here? He'd just rather stand on the deck below and yell up, "Who's driving now?"

Some lead by doing, by getting out in front where everybody can see you and paving the way. Others lead by barking out orders, standing on the sidelines of life, yelling, telling, imploring. General Eisenhower had noted that good leaders are out front pulling the string, not behind the line pushing it.

My father was both Grant and Vaughan. With his engineers he seemed to be leading by always telling them "There's no such word as CAN'T." Be a revolutionary. Don't live on the margins of life.

But at times he said, "Do as I say, not as I do," noting how the Greek philosophers like Plato and Socrates spoke of a sound body and mind. When sober his mind was as keen as those philosophers of Athens, but slowly he was losing his own bubble with brown bottles hidden around the house. He was like the silent, white caravels we'd encountered—his bright white facades controlled by the deeper, darker subsurface realities.

10. Scanning icebergs for signs of Little America

Chapter Five
Sea Life—Adelies, Weddells and Killers

Life in Antarctica millions of years ago was very different from what we observed steaming south through the pack ice.

We were surrounded by penguins, seals and killer whales, but many millions of years ago, Antarctica was located in a temperate zone.

Scott found a fossil fern named "Glossopteris" in the Trans Antarctic Mountains en route from the South Pole to his home base at Cape Evans, McMurdo Sound in 1912.

Byrd wrote me that they found enough coal in these same mountains to supply our country's fuel needs for many years. My grandfather loved telling me how coal forms from plant materials that decompose and sediment over millions of years. Without knowing it, this was my introduction to the carbon cycle that keeps our planet energized.

If there was coal, was there a possibility we might find oil, I had asked Byrd in my letter.

"You are entirely right about the possibility of finding oil in Antarctica" he had written.

And if there was oil perhaps one day people would want to drill for it as much as they do off the coast lines of America and in the Arctic regions.

And we now know that other animals once roamed the marshlands of this continent. One was a mammal like reptile named *Lystrosaurus*, a stout pig-like animal dwelling in swampy waters with eyes high atop his head. This creature was about four to five feet long, and had a barrel-like body low to the ground. Because we have found fossil remains of this creature in India and Africa as well, we conjecture that Antarctica was once joined to them over two hundred million years ago somewhere north of the south pole in a super continent called Gondwanaland.[7]

Another animal, probably a true dinosaur called *Cryolophosaurus* ("frozen crested lizard") had a two inch high forward facing crest atop its head, between the eyes, like the triceratops carnivorous dinosaurs you can see on display at The American Museum of Natural History in New York City. *Cryolophosaurus* was a theropod dinosaur, a true carnivore, looking like the later monster, TRex, that lived on Antarctica about one hundred and ninety million years ago.

Paleontologists wonder about the crests on these animals—What was their purpose? For defense? For attracting the opposite sex? We can never be certain, but upon seeing this crest, some observers dubbed the creature "Elvisaurus" after Presley's famous pompadour.

Life on this continent was very different during the lives of these two creatures. Antarctica is not what she seems. She is, in fact, a museum of early earth history encased in ice to a depth, in places, of more than two miles.

Now, on my first pack ice transit we began to see contemporary life abounding.

My first discovery was the Adelie penguin. This fifteen inch black and white bird waddled across the surface with its flippers flat out level with the ice looking like stabilizers for locomotion. The bird walks funny as kindergartners would say. And why, they ask? Because its feet are so short. The bird is mostly a creamy white chest made of feathers containing an oily substance that keeps them warm while swimming in the freezing waters.

Even though I had studied old black and white photos and read all the accounts from previous expeditions, I was still surprised by their behavior. It is one thing to read of these birds "tobogganing" across the ice, and quite another to witness their pushing forward with their strong webbed feet and pulling with their black flippers.

---

7   See Edwin H. Colbert, 1973 *Wandering Lands and Animals—The story of Continental Drift and Animal Populations.* New York: Dover Publications.

I was up in the bow leaning over the bulwark with my 8 mm camera taking pictures of these humorous critters when I first saw them toboggan away from the vessel as she broke up their playing fields.

Then came the event I had heard stories of from the old explorers, Adelies leaping out of the water onto the ice.

"How do they do that?" asked a sailor next to me.

"They propel themselves up from below the ice. What we can't see is that down below they're zooming around and when they want to surface, they point themselves upward and shoot through the surface of the water."

"Like a missile."

"Yeah, I guess so." Just like the ICBMs pointed at New York and Moscow on land and in our nuclear submarines.

When they wanted to return to the water to dive down and down so deep in search of food, the Adelies would line up on an ice foot staring into the dark waters. Their natural predators, whales and leopard seals, could be lurking down there so they had to be careful. They would wait and wait until one little fellow would push the first in line into the water. If he came up to the surface, then his playmates would peel off one by one like swimmers in an aquatic ballet diving into the freezing waters assured that the coast was clear.

All of a sudden the officer of the deck up in Loft Conn sent us dashing through a particularly narrow lead of ice sending ice and salt spray high over the ship's sides and we all got drenched.

"Sonofabitch!" yelled several crew members as they scurried away from the ship's sides getting sprayed with water and bits of splintery ice.

I looked up to Loft Conn to see who was driving but couldn't make out an image behind the rectangular windows reflecting the brilliant sun of the afternoon.

When Captains Ross and Scott sailed through these waters, they had to stop occasionally to "water ship." This involved selecting an ice floe where pressure had created little castles of ice called "hummocks" that could then be sliced and boxed up to be brought aboard and melted down. Scott noted,

> *As the pack ice is frozen sea-water, it may be a surprise to many that fresh water can be obtained from it, and it should be*

> *explained that for making the fresh water one does not take the ice itself but the snow which has fallen on its surface.*[8]

These adventurous mariners in their sailing vessels *Erebus* and *Discovery* looked for floes with significant pressure ridges to satisfy their thirst.

Perhaps Ross and Scott did not know that as salt water freezes it squeezes the salt from the surface down toward the lower regions of the forming ice floe so that much of the surface of sea ice is actually fresh water.

Glacier had huge condensers to transform sea water into fresh water so we had no need to stop to "water ship."

But we often came to a grinding halt in our progress through the pack due to impenetrable ice of the kind that Shackleton had encountered over in the Weddell Sea in 1915 when he became beset and, eventually, had to abandon the crushed *Endurance*. But, of course, *Glacier* could simply back down in her own wake, and charge the ice to overcome any stubborn plates of ice.

Unless, of course, we encountered ice conditions like those in the Bellinghausen in 1960 when *Glacier* became beset, stuck, for four days and men, officers and the Task Force Admiral resorted to all strategies, including prayer, to extricate themselves from their ice lock down. That was always a possibility I was nervous about. You didn't want to be the officer in charge that rammed the ship into a narrow lead only to become wedged in with pressures mounting on either side.

What was amazing to me at such times when we were rolling through various ice thicknesses was to discover the various colors of the ice. I'd always assumed that ice was white as in glaciers or transparent as in a glass of water.

But the underside of the pack ice formations was an amazing array of dark brown, yellow and reddish colors.

"What's all that?" I asked Doctor John Dinan, our medical officer.

Probably some kinds of diatoms, he said in his low, always commanding voice.

"What're they?" Having never taken biology in high school (only chemistry and impossible-to-understand physics), I had no idea what these undersea creatures were.

---

8   Captain Robert F. Scott 1905 *The Voyage of the 'Discovery'* Vol. 1, London: Smith, Elder & Co. p. 127

John described diatoms as microscopic plants, algae, and being a major source of food for fish and maybe penguins.

"They give off oxygen to the atmosphere," he added as we stood aft away from the bow where we could get an uninterrupted view of the scenery.

"How's that?"

"Photosynthesis," he said. "Don't you know *anything*?"

What I remembered after our conversation was that once my father had given me a chemistry set with something in it, a white powder I think, called "diatomaceous earth."[9]

"Was that the same thing?" I asked the doctor.

"Now, yer cookin' Johnny!" Dinan liked using that affectionate appellation for some reason. Ever since he reported aboard, I was "Johnny" to him and that was fine. No one else called me that and I realized that there are some people who immediately take liberties with your name and John Dinan was one of them. I never called him "Johnny," however. That didn't seem appropriate. He was a medical doctor, well over six feet tall and a very commanding presence on *Glacier*. John loved hanging out on the bridge, talking with Captain Grant and it often appeared to us as if he would love to command the ship in the ice from 'Loft Conn, and I'm sure he took his trick at the wheel from up there with Grant's encouragement.

And there were the seals, sleeping in the twenty-four hour sun, looking like my father on the day bed at 3:30 in the afternoon when everybody else was out working.

We would see them as a dark speck on the ice far off as we charged forward assuming that as *Glacier* got closer and closer they would wake up and lumber off. Their means of propulsion was even stranger than the Adelies. These creatures seemed to move by an internal self-propulsion mechanism that rolled their tons of blubber forward, snake-like, on a conveyor belt midway between tail and nose. Unlike the Adelies their flippers were of no use for this operation.

But strange to tell, they hardly ever moved away even though they could feel our surging 21,000 horses vibrating through the ice floes like nothing they'd ever experienced before. All the dark black Weddell seals did was lazily

---

9   Because diatoms have a cell wall made of silica (essential component of sand), this product was a good abrasive and, years ago, it was used in toothpaste.

raise their heads, look at this gray monster bearing down on them with an "oh so what" attitude, roll over and return to their drunken slumbers.

Finally, I saw my first whale. Not just any whale but a Killer Whale, also known as *"Orca gladiator"*, with its jet black body and tell-tale white bib tucked under its snout. They would sport about playfully in the leads porpoising in and out of the water showing us their smallish dorsal fins and hardly ever revealing their tails as do the much larger humpbacks up off the coast of California.

The Orcas had a "killer" reputation, as one of the scientists on board told us. When you capture one of them and slice it open, you were likely to find a wide array of different meals in various stages of digestion: from little Adelies, to Weddell and other seals. Scott and his men had many near disasters in the vicinity of *Orca gladiator*, among which was their photographer Herbert G. Ponting finding himself alone on an ice floe surrounded by hungry whales eager to make a meal of him. Fortunately for all of us, he escaped with his lenses in tact.

All of this sea life for a young man who never studied biology nor who ever fancied himself an animal lover, presented an abundance of surprises and delights. What I didn't give much thought to then was how it all represented the essence of "Nature, red in tooth and claw." Upon opening one *Orca* Scott and his biological team found

> *a seal, in the seal a fish, in the fish a smaller fish, in the smaller fish a copepod, and in the copepod a diatom. If this be regular feeding throughout, the diatom or vegetable is essentially the base of all.*

Indeed, those tiny brown little creatures on the underside of the pack ice were the foundation of the polar marine food chain.

Fortunately, I never saw a sea leopard, a smaller even more voracious animal, tear into one of the Adelie penguins ripping them so violently, after a taunting game of capture and escape, that they ripped their black and white tuxedoes right off their bloody bodies and sent it careening onto a nearby ice floe there to lie lifeless while the seal swallowed the gasping little fellow whole.

Killer whales and sea leopards were Nature's terrorists in the pack ice.

Chapter Five: Sea Life—Adelies, Weddells and Killers

Life in the pack was different from life at 23 Webster Park. There the only seals I had ever seen were small, plastic replicas hung around a bottle of booze, a bottle of "hooch," a fifth of Imperial Crown Whiskey. These little seals were all white except for a tiny red, round ball perched atop their uplifted noses. They were circus cute, but I detested them. I never collected nor played with them and hated to see them being brought into the house. I was always looking, not only for sex picture books in seventh grade, but also for these seals to empty into the trash can.

All plastic, tiny. artificial and revolting.

Now the seals I encountered were brown, weighing several tons, bewhiskered and sleepy regardless of the time of day. Some were lounging lollygaggers like the Weddells and others were vicious killers like the sea leopards. But they were all blubber, guts and power.

The animal life of Antarctica has evolved over hundreds of millions of years from *Cryolophosaurus* to Adelie, Emperor and Killer (although not directly). What the next million years of evolutionary development will yield may depend upon how we humans care for and preserve this environment and that of the whole planet.

11. Author offering nest-building stones to Adelie penguins

12. . . . with a playful Weddell seal

13. Emperors on full-dress parade inspection

Chapter Six
The Immensity!

Standing on top of one of Antarctica's tiny islands within McMurdo Sound I could survey the grandeur of this landscape. This was my first Antarctic command, being in charge of a party of *Glacier* men and a Dutch naval officer assigned by the Naval Hydrographic Office to plot the exact location of Tent Island, a jet black volcanic island Captain Scott could see from Cape Evans in 1911.

I just stood amidst our international orange tents pegged into the black volcanic soil to take in the immensity of my surroundings.

Four hundred and eighty feet above sea level looking westward toward the Prince Albert Range of Mountains I felt like Captain Ross on his first sighting of these magnificent peaks looking like smaller versions of the Swiss Alps, bathed in stark beauty of black, white, brown and, occasionally, a tinge of reddish rust. Prince Albert was Queen Victoria's husband when Ross discovered this bay area and the grandeur I now beheld.

Their peaks cut low yet razor like lines into the blue sky with no one promontory claiming altitude's absolute victory.

Every afternoon the sun dipped close to the horizon and rose to a height of about 20 degrees shooting its rays across the earth's curvature and onto this jagged tableaux of white, orange and pink. When Robert Scott sledged among these mountains across McMurdo Sound, he noted all these colors as well as bands of "blood red"--iron ore of some kind, most likely, but still hard to imagine mountains in Antarctica being that color.

Nothing impressed me more than these primary and pastel colors in the late afternoon seen against the foreground of the jet black and soft volcanic soil of Tent Island.

Like all Antarctic travelers before me I realized just how close they looked, as if a day's travel would bring us there. My grandfather, a scientist who loved playing curiosity games with me, asking "What if?" and "Why?" would have asked if I wondered why that was so and then through Socratic questioning he would have led me to consider that the air's clarity and unfouled nature allowed them to appear a lot closer than they were. Scott noted that you could almost see the "wrinkles" of the snowy banks below each mountain from afar.

I wondered about the geologic age of these black-red power players thrusting above the low snowy foothills leading from McMurdo Sound and the surrounding glaciers, Ferrar and Koettlitz. Just when did subterranean forces move a Ross Sea plate into conjunction with the land forcing them up inch by slow inch toward the polar sky? Or perhaps it was a Pacific or Antarctic Plate so many eons ago and the vista I now beheld lay somewhere else, perhaps conjoined with Africa and Australia twenty degrees of latitude north in Gondwanaland, some two hundred million years ago when the climate was warmer. Perhaps even the polar regions at that time were a temperate zone. Some geologists have concluded that where the Equator is now was once covered by an ice sheet.

Earth is dynamic, a living planet, constantly changing, erupting, moving and changing its surface appearances. Antarctica is not what she seems. Like all other continents she has been drifting over the molten mantle one to two centimeters per year. One of our guests on this Operation Deep Freeze voyage was a geophysicist studying the mantle, that part of the planet's interior between the surface crust and the outer core. Geologists consider it in a solid, yet molten state; it is constantly moving, circulating in convection currents in a kind of plastic state. I'd never heard of the mantle and spent a few watches conversing with our guest sponsored by the National Science Foundation trying to understand why they would want to drill down into it, why they would want to send seismic signals through earth to discover what it was made of—to map earth's interior he said and, thereby, to understand the dynamics of plate tectonics.

Geophysics was to have been my major at Harvard but when I met my bespectacled graduate student advisor who looked like the typical science "wonk" and he told me the physics courses I needed to take, I walked out of his office in Weld Hall, across Harvard Yard and decided to drop any consideration of becoming a scientist.

Too terrifying.

To the west and directly above us stood what I thought was the only active volcano in Antarctica, Mt. Erebus, named after Captain Ross's ship. A strange name for a vessel, I thought. *Erebus*, the land of the dead, home for the tortured souls writhing in agony in the cauldrons of igneous fusion.

There was always a plume of white smoke streaming northwest giving us a good indication of the prevailing winds. We had to cut our channel for the supply ships on a precise course of 147 to allow the winds to sweep out the icy debris we created by breaking through the solid ice covering McMurdo Sound.

When Captain Ross first saw this volcano from the decks of *Erebus* in 1841, he noted fire and flames shooting skyward. Shackleton, when he encamped in McMurdo in 1907, also noticed flames shooting upwards from the craters of Erebus.

But we saw no fire, no flames, no lava flows spilling over the side. Should there be a violent eruption, we'd all be wiped out in a surge of flaming lava pouring over the sides of this giant like hot fudge down the slopes of a vanilla sundae.

I wondered when she had been born in relation to the sharp peaks to the west. There must have been several geologic ages in between their births, or perhaps subterranean forces had moved one closer to the other inch by glacial inch and now we have on the one side baby mountains with their barbed peaks and Erebus with her so well worn down crater that she looked almost tired.

Southeast lay our ship's destination, Hut Point, and the McMurdo base of American scientists and naval personnel. Complete with a nuclear power plant, this base stood in stark contrast to the wooden huts Scott had erected there in 1901 and at Cape Evans in 1911. A long volcanic finger projecting into the Sound with a wooden cross 30 feet above the water line in reverence for one of Scott's men, Vince, who had lost his life in 1902 while out on a sledging party. Scott noted that this cross had been constructed "so firmly that I think in this undecaying climate it will stand for centuries."

Flying over to Tent Island in a CH-19 brilliant purple/orange helicopter piloted by Ltjg Al Kapocius and Lt. T. Dawson, I remembered my prior experience in mapping Antarctic waters at age fourteen. When I told my father I wanted to know where everything was, he suggested creating a model using plaster of Paris, but I thought drawing a chart would be better. And that's what we did one Saturday afternoon.

I recorded these recollections of that process in my journal:

> *Dad did all the hard work of finding the measurements of the Latitudinal and Longitudinal lines from the center circle. He spent a lot of time on that but finally attained perfect results...*
>
> *I started at approximaitly [sic] THE ROSS BARRIER and worked clockwise around the continent. Then I went over that with the colored pencils...I used blue for the coastline...After the coast line was complete I began work on the interior (mostly the mountains)...Next came the glaciers which I colored Yellow. Last came the huge portion of the Water. This was to be colored on the back of the map. The result was perfect so far as I was concerned...I didn't, however, fill in the Geographical lines with anything and that is the way it will be forever...*

(JB, typed, single spaced notes, dated several months after completing the chart, in 1953)

This chart introduced me to so many place names: Bellinghausen, Ross and Weddell Seas, Beardmore, Ferrar and Axel Heiberg Glaciers, Princess Astrid and Martha Coasts, mountains Grace McKinley and Fridtjof Nansen, and mountain ranges, Queen Maud, Rockefeller and Royal Society. Eventually, I learned how all of these people and societies had fostered polar exploration in years past. Here was my own private history lesson initiated with place names on a chart. For months I poured over my polar history books learning about Ross's and Bellinghausen's voyages thinking and feeling myself into the nineteenth century and imagining what it must have been like to be seeing these mountains, bays and glaciers for the first time.

Here was history as it was meant to be learned—from a deep fascination and curiosity about the lands, and the people who explored, settled, and struggled for survival on them. I never memorized any of the names nor the stories associated therewith because they became a part of my own story, my own adventure. I have lived imaginatively amongst all of these locations most of my life.

For years I kept this chart on a bulletin board covered in plastic, but recently my wife Nancy had the chart framed in burled walnut and it now hangs over my desk.

"Goddamit! I came over here to do what I'm good at!" shouted Lambert, our chief quartermaster as he vented his frustration that Captain Nielsen of the Danish Navy was taking more sightings than he was.

I tried to calm down this quartermaster so much larger than all of his subordinates. I told Lambert that the Commander was a guest and that he, Lambert, was really in charge of coordinating all the sightings. "You'll have to figure out where the hell we really are! Think about it! When we finally submit all these sightings to the Hydrographic Office, they'll have your name on them! You've got to determine where this wind blasted island is. It's up to you!"

Commander Nielsen's presence reflected the international nature of Antarctic exploration. We had visitors from Chile and other nations, countries interested in exploring the great white continent and *Glacier* provided them with the platform from which to launch their own investigations. Antarctica was, indeed, what Byrd had dreamed of—the site of international cooperation unlike any other in the world, a site of warm relationships among the scientific and naval support communities during the height of the intense cold war that raged between America and the Soviet Union. And *Glacier's* sea going complement of guests always wanted to sail on the biggest and most powerful polar vessel in the free world.

I'd received a D- in Navigation at Harvard because I couldn't do arithmetic calculations magnitude quickly and correctly. The pressure of figuring out star sights on paper in an examination room had forced me in to so many careless errors in adding and subtracting resulting in my almost bilging out, failing the whole program. D-!

Now I was responsible for fixing the position of a small island in McMurdo Sound. When Commander Swope, our Executive Officer, asked for a volunteer party to survey Tent Island for the US Hydrographic Office, I immediately stepped forward. They put their seal on all of our charts and here was a potential navigational aide to all sailors in the Sound if we could fix her position amongst the other volcanic islands surrounding her.

The command was mine and I couldn't help but think that so much of Harvard was just like that Navigation course, see what you can write down in forty minutes as if your future depended on it. But when you get into life as most people live it, you'll find there's usually a lot more time and people to help you figure things out--like where you are. Life wasn't an hour exam in Memorial Hall where you regurgitated all of the facts and figures you had memorized into the Blue Book regardless of whether or not it really answered the question. You just hoped that the exam reader would find enough clues there to assume you knew what you were talking about and give you a passing grade.

How inauthentic schooling is at times!

Our existence inside the tents was comfortable, if a bit crowded. After our survey sightings we would prepare a meal and attempt to keep the primus stove fires burning by using the protective screens to keep the wind from extinguishing them.

The evening meal was the big event of the day. The menu called for hot chocolate with or without those little floating marshmallow balls, canned stew by Dinty Moore, pemmican, rolls and canned fruit cup.

Our stew was perhaps not too far different from that Shackleton had brought to McMurdo in 1907--Moir's Army Rations (No. 1) "Consisting of Beef, Carrots, Potatoes, Onions and Gravy." Moir's had been awarded thirty one gold medals for excellence and was prepared in London, Paris, Vienna, Calcutta, New Orleans and Antwerp. This was probably quite a feast for the dauntless explorer who on that expedition would dash to within 97 miles of the South Pole and have to turn back to save the lives of his men. Imagine how often men in his party wondered about what might have been! Had they only brought enough trail rations, measured out their supplies differently or taken fewer men.

On a recent visit to Shackleton's hut at Cape Royds I had found these cans littered all around the exterior, just as he left them over fifty years previous. The signs said do not remove any relics from this shrine to the heroic explorers who pioneered in Antarctic exploration. But I figured I deserved to have one artifact and secretly removed one frozen can of Moir's Beef Stew and brought it back to the ship and sailed with it all the way to Boston.

Our stew was also different in one other remarkable fashion. It had been delivered in a cardboard carton by helicopter--there was no trekking over the bay ice, even the short 10 miles from where Glacier's heliport sat comfortably abaft the main mast. We also dined on the trail ration consumed by Shackleton, Scott, Amundsen and Byrd, that is pemmican. Byrd called this "compressed nourishment," comprised largely of fat, carbohydrates and protein. The body needs so much fat if high levels of energy are going to be expended. The composition we feasted on was made of prepared cereal, dehydrated beef liver (pre-cooked) dehydrated beef (pre-cooked), vegetable concentrate and hydrogenated vegetable oil.

When I bit into this thick cake-like pemmican, I remembered so many hours of reading about Scott and Byrd out on the trail where pemmican was the staple of their trail diet. Byrd noted that pemmican "is hardly a food for a fastidious man: it is greasy and rich; but explorers on the march, who are of necessity on reduced rations, soon come to look upon it as a food fit for the gods." [10] It tasted like a Christmas fruit cake with something added to make it richer, thicker and a little juicier. Perhaps it was the fat.

With each swallow of pemmican I became Scott out on the trail. I could taste the hurricane blizzards ripping at his green tents on a journey west of here up the Ferrar Glacier in 1903, pushing ever farther into the unknown territory of the polar plateau. With every crunch of that indigestion producing substance I could feel his thrill at struggling into the vast landscapes never before seen by humans, plateaus thick with ice down two miles to the hidden landscape.

---

10   Richard E. Byrd, 1930. *Little America.* New York: G. P. Putnam's Sons p. 35.

Chapter Six: The Immensity!   69

With every rumbling in my stomach I could sense the cramped quarters he and his geologist companions lived in, squished up together reading about Darwin's cruise on the *Beagle* during furious and numbing blizzards outside. As the pemmican slowly disappeared I remembered Scott's glowing description of what he was encountering,

> ...before us lay the unknown. What fascination lies in that word! Could anyone wonder that we determined to push on, be the outlook ever so comfortless?

After dinner I needed to get out and explore. In 1904 Scott had established a signaling system on Tent Island to give him adequate notice of the hoped for return of rescue ships. His ship *Discovery* had remained frozen in the Sound for a second winter further south at Hut Point where McMurdo Station was now located. He was anxious to return home and wanted to get word of a ship sighting as soon as possible. According to Scott's measurements the Island was 480 feet above sea level and I wanted to find out what there was to see beyond the slope on which our tents were pitched. So I told Lambert and Commander Nielsen I was going to reconnoiter.

Better take your ice ax, John. Never can tell when you might find a crevasse you need to crawl out of! Nielsen and Lambert grinned as I grabbed it just to make them happy. And off I trekked rather jauntily to satisfy my curiosity. As I started plodding across the windswept peak of this tiny island, all bundled up so there would be no possibility of frostbite, I recalled my first exploring expedition with my grandfather. Off to conquer the George Washington Bridge when I was about seven. He thought this would be a wonderful little trip, off to "cross over into another state," he said.

But when we got to the middle of the bridge, something happened. The bridge started to vibrate and I got very nervous.

I want to go home, I said.

My grandfather tried to explain to me that it was perfectly safe, even if we were bouncing up and down a little because of all the cars.

Look up at those cables, Johnny. Each one is full of hundreds and thousands of wires that are holding us up. There's no danger, as he held onto my hand tightly.

But I looked down at the water and became afraid of falling down over one hundred feet into the brown Hudson River.

It's really O.K. he said.

No, I said. I was frozen in fear right near the center span.

We never made it across to New Jersey. I think we tried it twice and I couldn't overcome my fear of bouncing up and down with the chills running up into my groin.

He was a good sport about it, not telling my grandmother, at least not in front of me. That had been my first opportunity to explore with my grandfather and I became terrified of rumbling automobiles suspended over the murky Hudson River.

Tent Island was my own little expedition, no bouncing up and down and no fear of the terrible -50 temperatures Byrd experienced at Advance Base and no crevasses to swallow you up. This was just a little sight seeing jaunt. . .souvenir hunting. . .gazing over toward Cape Evans. . .No fear of our tents breaking off and floating to certain death in the Ross Sea as I'd imagined back in Claire Slattery's English class when I wrote "Twenty Below." That was an imaginary command where, because of a widening crevasse on the Ross Ice Shelf, we faced the ultimate danger of calving off and becoming a floating iceberg adrift in the Ross Sea during the dead of winter. A fate that I had to save my imaginary expedition from.

As I strolled merrily about the black almost dusty volcanic slopes of the island, I felt as if I had finally begun to live out the dreams woven out of isolation, boredom and anger not so many years ago. Now it was about 10 degrees F. outside with prevailing light breezes from the south east. Without many clouds it was a brilliant blue sky with color all around.

Off to the north east and not many miles away were other volcanic islands—the Delbridge Islands--Inaccessible and Big and Little Razorback. All were jet black with steep slopes sliding down to the glistening blue-white bay ice surrounding them. Inaccessible was higher than Tent Island and a couple of miles distant. It was between these two islands that one of Scott's men, Atkinson, got lost during the winter night of 1911 while out reading thermometers; he suffered frostbite and burrowed into the volcanic soil for safety from the blizzard snows. Fortunately, he made it back to base camp at Cape Evans just four miles away.

Towering above me were the glistening slopes of Erebus, the active volcano that must have exploded so many thousands of years ago the way Mauna Kea, and Mona Loa have recently done in the creation of the Hawaiian Island chain. Millions of years ago flaming lava poured over the crater's edge and down into the surrounding waters sending plumes of steam hundreds of feet into the air creating and extending the land, just the way Kilauea does now.

With every step I felt a deep excitement never before experienced, as if I could discover something of scientific value. Here was uncharted territory, at least for me, with no fears of running afoul of undetected obstructions or of falling off into the waters below. It felt like my first Christmas when I ran down the corridor from my room toward the living room sure that I had heard Santa Claus's reindeer up on the roof earlier that night. The thrill was enhanced when I discovered my first train set—jet black engine with red and yellow cars on a figure eight track layout Santa Claus must have spent some time putting together. Now, how'd he do that? And the cookies were, indeed, gone.

As I wandered, I wondered if I might find some remnants of Scott's men, perhaps some food cartons, a cache of provisions left in hasty retreat after the rescue ship *Morning* finally broke through the bay ice to embark Scott and his men for the long voyage back to England in 1904. Maybe a glove or parts of the signaling system he had been left behind.

I also recalled that during the deep darkness of winter in July and August 1911 Scott permitted three of his men, Dr. Wilson, "Birdie Bowers" and Apsley Cherry-Garrard to undertake a daring journey from Cape Evans around the southern slopes of Mt. Erebus to the Emperor penguin rookery at Cape Crozier.

So three men set out in the dark to determine if Emperor penguin embryos showed any indication of teeth, evidence that might link them with primitive birds, early reptiles and, perhaps, even dinosaurs. Wilson reasoned that if present day birds had ever had teeth they would show up in the embryos of "the most primitive birds living now"--perhaps like the vestigial tail humans are known to possess in embryo.

That Wilson linked penguins with dinosaurs I found utterly fantastic. How could he see a connection between those giant saber-toothed lizards like Tyrannosaurs Rex and our little Emperor penguins?

Cherry-Garrard called this "the weirdest bird's nesting expedition that has ever been or ever will be." [11]

Their experiences were adventurous in the extreme. As I trundled across the fine jet black lava dust I saw visions of those three men enduring -70 temperatures in the dark, taking hours to get into their frozen-like-cast-iron-clothes, picking their way so carefully through treacherous crevasses aided only by the moon and having to use two boxes of matches just to light their primus stove in the evening. The aurora was always before them as they traveled east. "Now most of the sky was covered with swinging, swaying curtains which met in a great whirl overhead: lemon yellow, green and orange."

When they finally got around Erebus, past Mt. Terror to Cape Crozier, they found the rookery and salvaged three Emperor eggs for the British Museum.

Meanwhile what I found on Tent Island were skua gulls in broad daylight, a whole airborne squadron of them suddenly circling about my head with intentions that were not altogether clear. These brown creatures, it seems, were following me on my meanderings and I was still oblivious of where I was going.

Suddenly one of them broke away from its circling squadron and just like a Grumman Hellcat taking a bead on an enemy submarine in the North Atlantic the bird swooped down toward me with its beak penetrating the chill of an Antarctic evening. I saw him coming and was startled by his flight path. What the hell is he doing? And I hoisted my ice ax in self-defense, just as he pulled out at six inches above my head.

Godalmighty! What is this?

And then the whole squadron followed the lead of the top gun. They all ceased their circling and started swooping down on me, one after another and now I was walking around in circles because these rapacious birds had a strategy. They didn't just come down in one line. No, they were too seasoned as attackers for that maneuver. They kept me off balance and out of stride by coordinating their swoops from all directions of the compass.

---

11 Apsley Cherry-Garrard, 1922 *The Worst Journey in the World, Antarctic, 1910-1913*. London: Penguin Books Limited, Chapter VII.

Chapter Six: The Immensity!

                          12 o'clock high
10 o'clock
flash   3 o'clock strike
                          6 o'clock
                          swipe

What the hell are they after?

Look out! Here come two of them now! They've changed their tactics. God! How many of them are there? I just kept turning and ducking and turning and stumbling and lost all sense of direction. By now I was almost desperately attempting to return to camp and the safety of my companions who would surely help me fend off the brown bombers.

As I reached the top of one hill, I looked hopefully for the bright red-purple tents, but saw only more birds swooping down upon me, some even lowering their landing gear hoping, I suppose, to set down and feast. I poised my ice ax like a Nike anti-ballistic missile to prevent this. None of them got close enough to lose a feather. Too cunning for that! But I was lost again, lost out on a volcanic island with slopes and horizons all about me unable to find my way home thereby breaking a cardinal rule of polar travel—Never Travel Alone! How many times had I read that? Of explorers roped together?

The birds continued their relentless onslaught swooping and zooming down toward my green foul weather cap as I stumbled from one gentle rise to another. Goddamn! Where are the tents? Where's Lambert?

I was lost in the middle of an island on the coast of Antarctica and there was no test I could have taken to figure out where I was. Like Byrd on one of his winter jaunts from Advance Base in 1934 when he lost the trail of his footprints—you had to use the stars or the sun to figure out a logical direction home.

Eventually, I came puffing into our little camp, having successfully retreated from what I imagined to be the jaws of imminent danger.

The truth came out later back on board the ship when one of our visiting biologists told me that even though Mother Nature endowed skuas with a completely guiltless need to swoop down, steal and devour penguin chicks, it provided them with a way of defending their young: by attacking those who wandered too close to their nesting spots. I had unwittingly come too close to their own colony of nursing mothers and their dive bombing was an instinctive self-protection strategy. They guarded their homes from intrusion by unwelcome visitors.

Once back aboard *Glacier* after the Tent Island adventure, I poured a cup of steaming hot coffee, took a long, non-regulation shower and thought about Wilson, Bowers and Cherry-Garrard and their egg hunting adventure.

I lay on my bunk on top of crisply clean white sheets with a pillow pumped up by one of our stewards thinking about their ordeal, wondering why they went and how they really survived:

While encamped in a stone hut of their own crafting at Cape Crozier they nearly lost their tent in winds of such monstrous fury that Cherry-Garrard "wondered why it did not carry away the earth." Without their tent they surely would have died on the return journey. Low on fuel and numb from the cold, frost-bite, sleeping in bags as stiff as the igneous rocks formed deep within Erebus, they slogged through Nature's worst hell never imaginable by two of my favorite high school authors, Puritan preacher Jonathan Edwards and James Joyce in *A Portrait of the Artist as a Young Man*.

How in the world, I wondered, did he keep his mind straight, away from dreaming about being back in London with friends, family and a beloved?

> *I invented a formula. . .which I repeated to myself continually. . . I used to seize the shovel and go on digging [repeating to myself] 'You've got it in the neck. . .Stick it--stick it--stick it--stick it. . .'*

This formula saved Cherry-Garrard, but I would have had such a time trying to hold onto the shovel at -65 degrees! Out wandering about near 23 Webster Park trying to get frostbitten years ago I noticed that in below freezing temperatures, my fingers wandered away from each other and when I tried to write down a few notes in my ice caves, I couldn't even hold the pencil! How in the world did Scott and his men manage to keep such extensive journals while freezing to death? And I couldn't hold the pencil tightly!

And why did they do this?

Chapter Six: The Immensity!

> *We traveled for Science. Those three small embryos from Cape Crozier were striven for in order that the world may have a little more knowledge, that it may build on what it knows instead of on what it thinks.*

These three endured burning, biting cold without their beloved sugar--especially peaches in luscious, thick syrup awaiting them at Cape Evans--in order to find out, to explore the mysteries of Emperor penguin evolution.

What fascination lies in that word! Unknown.

All for truth enshrouded in a terrifying Crozier mystery. Truth derived from evidence grudgingly acquired during "the worst journey in the world." They were intensely curious about nature, wanting to discover its true story and not to live with myth, supposition or assumption.

Their truth lay in a possibility, the possibility of penguin's teeth. Today, we know that Wilson was correct in his hypothesis—there is a link between dinosaurs and birds and chickens. Indeed, today we think of chickens as "theropod dinosaurs," sharing several characteristics with some dinosaurs—three toed feet, a breastbone, hollow bones, even feathers and the hole in the hip socket allowing upright movement. How prescient Wilson was—linking dinosaurs with today's birds, albeit with different reasoning.

Wilson and his companions challenged themselves with "What if. . ?" questions, refusing to be shackled by their own or others' limiting assumptions, striving in the midst of horrific blizzards and sub-zero temperatures for nature's elusive truths—"for Science."

Balls to the wall! Full steam ahead!

But lying there in my warm bunk with coffee still warm from the wardroom, I felt the yawning division between Wilson and my father--the record of companionship that all members of this party lived to tell, if only briefly:

> *These two men [Wilson and Bowers] went through the Winter Journey and lived: later they went through the Polar Journey and died. They were gold, pure, shining, unalloyed. Words cannot express how good their companionship was,*

Here were men you could always rely on, steadfast in the face of terrible and cruel winds that sapped their strength to the point that they wished they would just slip into a deep, dark crevasse and disappear. Here were men of character, like Byrd and Joe DiMaggio. Men you could always rely on when you were hanging onto the lip of a coffin-like crevasse in a howling blizzard. Men who would lend you their warm flesh when you were suffering from frostbite. . .

> Men of gold. . .pure, shining, unalloyed. . .
> Solid of stripe

We sent the data from Tent Island to the US Naval Hydrographic Office in Washington, DC . On their 1965 (Rev. 1978) Chart—29321—of Franklin Island to McMurdo Sound (including Ross Island and the Prince Albert Range), you can find Tent Island demarked with a black dot in the center indicating its precise location on earth at 77 degrees 41.2 minutes South Latitude, 166 degrees, 21.7 minutes East Longitude.

Make your mark on the charts.

Be sure you investigate to gather the data, the facts, before drawing conclusions. Observe, think, ask good questions and figure things out. "We went for science. . . " Build on what you know, not what you *think* you know.

14. Tent Island explorations

Chapter Seven
"Don't try, Dammit! Do it!"

My grandfather suffered through a terrible childhood difficulty, stuttering. Life in school as he described it was "just plain Hell." Sometimes he would be the only one who knew the answer to a teacher's question, but he refused to raise his hand for fear of "stammering," as he sometimes called this malady. When selected valedictorian of his ninth grade graduation class, he was asked to write and deliver a graduation speech. He grew up not far from Rochester, New York in a little town called LeRoy near Lake Erie. And even though his family promised him a Great Lakes cruise, he refused to speak in front of his friends on graduation day.

When a classmate read my grandfather's words, Llewellyn Ray Ferguson sat in the audience mortified at the terrible way the alternate stumbled through the speech.

As my aunt Anne tells this story it was only through his persistence that he thereafter overcame this handicap. "He made himself give oral reports and recitations; anything that would put him in a spot where he had to talk in front of a group." Gradually, he overcame his difficulty and when he entered Cornell, there was no trace of stuttering in his speech. He took control of his situation the way Cherry-Garrard had: "Stick it!" Imagine your success and pursue it with persistence. Never give up.

My own difficulties when first reporting to the Antarctic fleet of icebreakers was a little different. Captain Grant loved to hear about Admiral Byrd and his doings, but when it came to ship operations he could become a raging tiger.

Chapter Seven: "Don't try, Dammit! Do it!"

"God damn it to Hell! Barell." Capt. Grant screamed so many times into my ears. "Why can't we talk to those helicopters?" It didn't matter that I had only been onboard *Glacier* for four weeks, I was now responsible for all of the radio equipment as Communications Officer.

"Damn it all! We can't hear what the hell those helos are saying and they're only a few fucking feet in the air!" he said pointing off to starboard where the bright international orange helicopter #82 hovered over the ice about to fly out in search of open water.

It didn't matter that this problem must have originated months, perhaps years, ago. It was now my responsibility to ensure that radio operators could read signals from the pilots "five by five," as they said, or "loud and clear."

"I'll try to find out, Captain," I told him up on the bridge without any idea of what to do, feeling confused by the whole situation. I had no idea in the world what to do about those radios. Most of my prior experience involved turning them on and off, and spinning the dials looking for "The Lone Ranger" after dinner or finding Notre Dame football on a Saturday afternoon. My only mechanical experience came in working with my grandfather to build the crystal set that pulled radio signals out of the air in Hartsdale (NY) and transmitted them into a set of black earphones I wore under the covers at night. Granddaddy had explained how radios work as I spoke so excitedly with him about my discoveries. I heard the crackling of the atmosphere as I moved the needle over the granite like crystal searching for New York stations. Back when I was eight years old it already seemed as if I were at sea listening to short wave broadcasts. The straight steel pointer, poised over the round, shiny crystal, looked like a strange silver feeler from a South American butterfly just sitting there exploring out the surface with its long proboscis for its own protection or sustenance.

I'll try to find out, I said standing by his captain's leather chair on the bridge.

"Don't *try!* Dammit! *Do* it!"

Grant sounded so much like my father. "Just get it done! That's what I have to tell those engineers constantly--every time they say, 'Ralph, it just can't be done!'

"That drives me crazy, John. CAN'T. That word ruins your mind and ought to be banished from the English language! There's no such word as CAN'T..."

Back in the early 1950s the telephone always seemed quite adequate to me, but Ralph James Barell saw the potential in this machine called a "computer" and he urged his engineers to stretch their thinking beyond current and self-imposed limitations, and press forward toward the kinds of innovation concurrently being developed by James Watson at IBM.

My father was a not so quiet revolutionary around our house, and often unappreciated by his family. None of us, neither my older sister nor my mother put him in the same category as Thomas Edison, Alexander Graham Bell or Albert Einstein. But he was an imaginative visionary captivated by possibilities only a few could see.

Captain Grant never minced words and was not interested in what he denounced as "goddamned excuses," only positive results and the quicker the better. You always knew what he wanted done; there was seldom any equivocation or ambivalence.

Ed Grant had been a boxer at California State College and he looked it, wiry, lean and trim, no fat around the gut. When one of my fellow officers, Henry Ohls, entered the Captain's cabin with a radio message as we were rolling our way south in the Roaring Forties, he found Ed Grant in his working khakis down on deck doing push ups. Always stay in fighting trim.

"I can do better with a goddamn bull horn on the port wing of the bridge," he would say gesturing out toward the two orange helos suspended in the deep blue Antarctic sky. On such occasions I could even detect a slight grin amidst his justifiable anger.

It didn't take long to figure out the problem: the ultra high frequency radio equipment was worn out. I had a hard time swallowing this, because it always seemed to me that a ship belonging to the US Navy had what was necessary to do its mission. It had the best equipment there was, no questions asked. This was my first lesson in the reality of dealing with government operations. When reporting for duty aboard the ship, I also discovered that the green foul weather jacket I'd brought from my previous ship was better than anything they had aboard *Glacier*. It had the word "COCKE" spelled out in block letters on the back and I wondered if that described physiology or temperament, or both. (I still have this jacket and, even though the plastic zipper chafes, it still fits.)

Chapter Seven: "Don't try, Dammit! Do it!" 81

"Why can't we get new ones?" I asked our first class radioman, Perkins.

"We've put in orders after the last two cruises and nothing happens," he said.

"Why?" I asked in ignorance.

"I dunno. I guess they think we can get along by jury rigging these."

A "jury rig" (or jerry rig) was a patch up job without standard Navy issue parts that could be pretty bizarre. In an old Cary Grant movie, "Operation Petticoat," a Navy Wac repaired a submarine's circulation pump with a girdle much to the utter dismay of the chief machinist.

Nothing at Harvard or its NROTC program had prepared me for this kind of problem. All I seemed to do in so many of my courses was create mindless mnemonics, nonsense words that helped you, under examination pressure, to remember significant-to-the-professor facts or ideas: "**M I R A M A R**" stood for a bunch of facts in one of Professor Wolf's courses in Russian History, stuff to be ingested like those spelling/vocabulary words at the bottom of my rough draft letter to Admiral Byrd, meaningless matter just lying there to be memorized and regurgitated upon demand.

When I arrived in the fleet and began serving on board *Mauna Kea*, I kept looking for a manual to tell me how to solve the problems of first class bosun mates tattooed from head to toe wanting to go on liberty at 8 a.m. in the morning to continue drinking all day and first class electricians who let the electric powered fork lift trucks used to move 500 pound bombs die out from lack of battery charging. I was terribly naive, always reverting to bookish tendencies when confronted with these real-world quagmires. I even thought that *US Navy Regulations* might contain some kind of answer, so used was I to looking up specific answers in books.

But neither Harvard nor my public school education had given me much preparation in solving problems that arise from the dailiness of life. Whatever problems we did solve had a "yes, you're absolutely right" answer often in the back of the Teacher's Edition. In high school World History I had a running contest with John Canoni to see who could memorize more information about Mazzini, Garibaldi and his Red Shirts and Cavour as they struggled for and against unification of the provinces of Italy in the mid nineteenth century. The more information you chocked into your memory banks, the higher your score on Mae Millikin's examinations. We goaded each other with exam scores that read 103% or 104% Stuff it all in there. Problem solving in mathematics, from algebra to calculus was designed to find the value of an "x" that bore no relationship to me, Wellesley or life as I knew it.

Not so out in the fleet.

"Don't they understand what's goin' on here?" I asked Perkins about the bureaucrats in Washington in all my innocence.

"Oh, they don't give a shit," he said. "They think all they gotta do is outfit the ship, let it slide down the ways and then sail off into the sunset. They're desk jockeys who have no idea what it's like to try to hammer out a signal through an amplifier held together with tubes pirated from a goddamned *radar*."

"Now, Mr. Barell your presence is requested on the bridge!"

Oh, shit! Not again! Goddamn those pilots! Why don't they just play cards in the hangar deck some more? I was getting sick of all these calls to the bridge that always reminded me of a principal calling you down to his office because you'd been doodling or whispering in the back row. I'd been up to the bridge so many times because of these rotten old radios that men at the helm looked at me in pity.

Fellow officers laughed about my ass being full of buck shot!

What's going on now? How am I going to get him off my back? This is almost as bad as standing watch in front of the blazing hot ship's boilers on my first midshipman cruise ship, the heavy cruiser *Albany*.

"Yes, sir!" I said saluting Captain Grant as he sat in his Captain's leather chair staring out across the pack ice stretching clear across the horizon. I knew he was going to chew me out for another failure. All I could do was come prepared to tell him what we were already doing, patching in one radio with another and hoping for the best.

"We just can't live like this, John." I was surprised at his tone of voice, calm, deliberate as if we were again on that first watch and he was keeping my mind off the ship's rolling 30 degrees and churning up my stomach so I puked ever hour on the hour.

"We just have to find a solution besides these goddamned jury rigs. O.K.?"

"Yes, sir!" I said, still not knowing what to do.

Chapter Seven: "Don't try, Dammit! Do it!"

But from somewhere, perhaps the den where my father listened incessantly to Mendelssohn's soaring violin melodies, I realized you had to think beyond the stuff of the day, the normal routines that governed or choked our imaginations. Do something different. Imagine the possibilities. Go beyond the immediate horizon.

Go to the source!

Think success! See it!

Balls to the wall!

When we returned to Boston, I decided I had to go to Washington, to the Bureau of Ships. This idea came to me perhaps because I remember my second visit with Admiral Byrd.

This time I was greeted not by Byrd himself but by his secretary Gladys Wood. After I rang the bell, I looked in through the marvelous dark wood and glass door into the vestibule.

"You must be John," she said opening the door. "Please, come in. The Admiral is in the next room with some reporters." I could hear the slight whirr of cameras and, eventually, Byrd joined me with a companion whom he introduced as "Dusty," a naval officer I thought had been with him on the second expedition, Frederick G. Dustin.

We rode in an official haze gray government car to the pier in Boston harbor where USS *Atka* was about to set sail for Antarctica to explore bases for the forthcoming Operation Deep Freeze and the International Geophysical Year.

En route to Boston harbor his secretary Miss Wood sat between John F. Barell, high school student at the time and Rear Admiral in the United States Navy, Richard Evelyn Byrd. As we settled in for the ride with "Dusty" and the navy driver up front, Byrd said Miss Wood was "like a rose between two thorns." At that moment Byrd had elevated me to his equal. I was one of the "thorns." [12]

---

12   In reviewing my files of correspondence from 9 Brimmer Street I find many letters from Miss Wood thanking me for writing the Admiral, explaining that "Admiral Byrd has been away for the past two months and is still away. . .As he is not able to attend to his mail while traveling, your letter will be held here until his return. I know he is always glad to hear from you and appreciates your deep interest in exploration." (2/9/53)

There I was, Admiral Byrd's guest standing on the pier listening to him give a press conference with Commander Jacobsen, *Atka's* skipper. I took notes and photographs and felt that resurgence of pride, joy and surprise and my being there. But then they went aboard ship and I lost them. I searched the ship from stem to stern, from mess decks up to the bridge, but there was one place I failed to investigate, the ship's wardroom. I failed to knock on the door from some fear of being rejected. I knew all I had to do was tell the officer that I was Admiral Byrd's guest and I'd be ushered in. But I failed to raise my hand, make a fist and knock on that door.

To this day I am chagrined, embarrassed and perplexed by this failure to knock on that door. I still shudder to think what Byrd thought of his young guest on the ride back to 9 Brimmer Street when I told him of this mishap.

Well, he's no Paul Siple, the Eagle Scout with him on his First Expedition. Not fit for polar duty.

How I could have grown up to be so shy, reticent and fearful in some circumstances, but not in others? This was and still is a major mystery to me. Some experiences, like this one, write indelible messages into your memory creating negative models you vow never to repeat. This was first and most powerful Never Again Experience.

So I decided in the summer of 1963 to go to Washington and knock on a few doors

The Lieutenant at the "BuShips" was not sympathetic and put up the usual resistance at first, saying "How can I do this for you and not for *Atka* or *Staten* or *Burton Island*?"[the other, smaller icebreakers on this voyage.]

"How can the flagship of the fleet not be able to talk with her own helos on a dangerous rescue mission? How can we host the Commodore and miss important messages?" I replied immediately leaning across the desk. "We had His Eminence Cardinal Cushing on board last cruise. Suppose he needed to be airlifted ASAP and we couldn't communicate? What then?"

"We just don't have these things lying around here you know? You have to go through channels," he said leaning way back in his chair with an enigmatic smile as if he were toying with me.

"We *have*--here are copies of all the DD-1140s we've sent in so far." I lay the Navy's standard requisition slips out on his desk, all signed by Captain Grant in a firm, determined hand. Like Apsley-Cherry Garrard and Edmund

Wilson out looking for penguin teeth at Cape Crozier I had sought out and found the data, the evidence.

But to no avail. What had happened to all of these requests for assistance, each telling a story of missed opportunities, lost communications, not meeting responsibilities?

That sent him further back in his chair for a moment. He gazed for an answer at the color photos on the wall of an aircraft carrier, a tin can and a black and white photo of the Japanese surrender on the battleship *Missouri*.

You can repair what you've got, he kept saying as if I were asking for a loan from his personal bank account.

Dodge and stall. . .that seemed to be the order of the day. Don't meet the problem head on, just find a way to wiggle out of your responsibility.

I explained that we'd been doing that for years already—that we've been cannibalizing everything, including the damned radars in order to keep the airwaves alive. We're not making any progress.

I thought about pulling out the Admiral Byrd card from my deck and saying, "Look at that picture on your wall. Do you know who *that* particular admiral is standing in the row of flag officers next to MacArthur on the *Missouri* in Tokyo Bay in 1945? Well, I do and I've met him and he's the reason I'm on this "most powerful breaker, the ship that served as his flagship in 1956."

I pressed the lieutenant like a thorn in his side.

"C'mon Lieutenant do you want us out there freezing our asses off yelling into the damned bull horns at helicopters screeching over head? Now how does that look to a Commodore? And besides," I said taking a deep breath and leaning back in my chair, "my name will be lower than whale shit if I don't get something from you." Somewhere along the way, perhaps from Harvard, maybe from the ammunition ship *Mauna Kea* or possibly from the oiler's million dollar collision at sea, I had developed this cock-sure attitude when dealing with certain officers. With a few drinks in me in Alameda California while on liberty with shipmates at the Naval Air Station I would joke and none too quietly poke fun at the captains sitting across the bar, especially if they were "airdales" (pilots) or "jar heads" (marines).

"Is that what it's come to?" He straightened up and once again produced that enigmatic smile.

"O.K. I'll see what I can do."

When? How? Once you had him hooked, even a little, you couldn't risk allowing him to slither off like a feisty Adelie penguin out of the jaws of killer leopard seal. Reel him in, bag it and close the deal!

"I'll get you two UHF transmitters from our reserves."

I knew it! They always had something in stock--just like the hotel clerk who finds you a room after declaring he's all booked up-- and why hadn't they honored our previous requests? I didn't ask.

A marginal imagination right here in Washington!

Persist, Damn it! There's no such word as. . .

There seemed to be an arrogance of power on the part of those so far removed from the daily world of the fleet where your screws churned up real water, where we all stood watches in the middle of a limitless plane of the sea at midnight with cups of black coffee sludge hooked onto our right index fingers and where a ship's bow plunging deeply into oncoming waves could roil your stomach into spasms of sea-green sickness.

Washington wasn't the real world of fleet operations.

People at headquarters were what we in the fleet called "desk jockies," men and women who had either done their service on water or weren't qualified. In any event, they seemed to run the Navy to suit their own purposes. Yes, they had budgets, quotas and limited resources, but deep in the pack ice we had to complete a mission; we had to get the job done with no questions asked. To do that we needed the best equipment the US Government could provide and we no longer had it after eight years of continuous pounding through the ice in and around Antarctica.

Men at the Bureau of Ships seemed out of touch, like school administrators and CEOs of large corporations who knew little of what was going on where the real work of the organization was occurring, where the tire tracks meet the road, at the coal face. They were isolated and, perhaps, not accustomed to getting their fingers frost-bitten or greased up alongside the men and women on the factory floor.

Washington is the command center where life and death policy decisions are made by a few for the rest of us in the fleet and at home. But leaders without operational experience sometimes risk the lives of those of us in the field, in peace time and in combat.

Inoperable radios and insufficient, ragged foul weather gear told a tale of neglect that could have lead to disaster and loss of life. Poorly armored vehicles in time of war, be it defensive or pre-emptive, can mean immediate death to those driving around in them on foreign soil and it just isn't sufficient to be told that it is a matter of the physics of production. Scrounging around for bailing wire or "hillbilly armor" during times of emergency is worse than poor planning. It verges on the criminal.

"Make you plan and work your plan" my father always said.

If, as Kennedy said in his inaugural, this was our hour of maximum danger and international challenge, we needed more power output, more reliability, sufficient equipment and education to complete the mission.

Keep knocking on doors

Chapter Eight
Bud Waite and the Truth

In the end we received even more radios from another, unexpected source, one of the men who rescued Byrd from Advance Base in 1934, Amory H. "Bud" Waite, a real Antarctic veteran from the heroic age of exploration.

When visiting *Glacier* during the summer after my first cruise, Bud asked me if we needed anything. He then worked at an Army Communications Center in New Jersey and would be embarking for our next Deep Freeze cruise.

I told him about the terrible condition of the radios and, without any hesitation, without any DD 1140s, he brought another UHF transmitter/receiver thereby increasing our overall capacity by fifty percent.

Doors opening

He also brought along a little polar scooter, one of the first snowmobiles in existence, designed for recreational travel across the ice at high speeds or, more likely, for hauling sledges full of scientific gear to a remote outpost.

In November, Bud sat across from me at a table in the wardroom as we continued to break the channel through the ice toward Hut Point. We were now on my first full cruise from Boston, through the Panama Canal, across the Pacific to Christ Church, New Zealand and again through the Roaring Forties and Furious Fifties. This time I didn't puke my guts up on the first hint of rolling seas. I'd lived with the watermelon bottom for long enough and had earned and acquired my "sea legs." They were now strong and flexible on the tossing, pitching deck thereby building up my calf and thigh muscles to a full back's level of conditioning.

Bud looked to be in his sixties, still sporting the mustache he wore in Little America in 1934, balding and with large, weathered hands that had been frost bitten so many times from exposure to frozen generators in the minus seventy degrees of the Antarctic night. Here sitting across from me was the first "Old Antarctic Explorer" any of us in the wardroom had ever met. Here was somebody who had experienced those tiny white spots of frostbite and lived to tell the story.

Bud loved to reminisce about his days with Admiral Byrd. He recalled sailing on the *Bear of Oakland* in 1933 as a young radio operator.

"That ship tossed and rolled so much I had to brace my self real good." He described sitting at the Morse code key with his back up against one of the ship's main wooden masts sunk deep within the hull and pressing his feet against the bulkhead [interior wall].

"D'you ever get sea sick tossing around like that?"

"Naw! Are you kidding? We'd roll 30 or 40 degrees and I'd be banging out all sorts of messages back to New Zealand and to other ships--no, I was in my element then." He reminded me of my father's descriptions of flying DC-3s over Louisiana in a storm. "Like being on a bucking bronco!" he said. And he loved it too, imagining himself as the star of the rodeo wearing his white cowboy hat.

As Bud spoke my imagination once again swirled down and around that magical triangle created by the radio towers, those beacons of steadfastness and hope within a community of adventurers. I could hear the bongos of my favorite song from those days in 1952 of fantasizing about Little America, "Delicado" banging in the background. The bongos, the harpsichord and then the soaring violins of this three minute Percy Faith rendition created an enchanting song that sent me soaring off into a fantasy world of magic and mystery.[13] I played it so many times that members of my family, like my cousin Sally, often asked me if I'd rather have a grilled peanut butter sandwich or listen to "Delicado."

Both, I said.

---

13 "Delicado" was composed by Brazilian artist Valdir Azevedo, recorded by Percy Faith, among many others, and reached No. 1 on the Billboard charts in 1952.

Delicado. "Delicate and dainty?" Hell, no! Full power down to the triangle!

As Bud told me about climbing to the top of one of these steel towers to affix a propeller for his radio generator, I saw the old photographs, the footsteps in the snows leading from the left foreground, those mysterious footprints of one unknown explorer who had been off on a stroll, a promenade for fresh air or for fresh seal meat. Bud's words awakened so many dormant images, of the polar flight, of Lawrence Gould's dog sled teams mushing across the Barrier through the Valley of Crevasses on toward the Queen Maud Mountains there to gather evidence of Antarctica's geological evolution, the seams of coal, the fossilized ferns, *Glossopteris,* more evidence of the continent's tropical past. Where did he think Antarctica had been millions of years ago? I'm not a geologist, he said, but somewhere else because how else would we have these petrified plants?

After Byrd settled in at Advance Base, he began a routine of taking weather "obs" as he called them, climbing out of his 9 x 12 hut buried in the Ross Ice Shelf due south of Little America.[14] He'd gone there to find out what connections existed between Antarctic weather and that of the rest of the world. Byrd was a pilot in the Navy, used to taking weather into account, avoiding it, always taking its measure. But what led him to this hypothesis?

Life at Advance Base was perilous in the extreme. Once he went for a stroll after taking his readings, turned around and discovered that he was lost. Had no idea which way was home. Then his naval aviator training kicked in and he plotted out expanding searches in all directions and, finally, picked up his tracks not yet snowed over.

On another occasion he made his observations and returned to the trap door down into his warm hut. But it was frozen solid. No way to enter. He almost panicked for fear of freezing to death. Eventually, he found a shovel he accidentally left topside and pried open the door. "Luck" favors the prepared mind.

Reading these exploits in his book *Alone* back in seventh grade left me in awe of his abilities to survive amidst the harshest conditions on the planet. I never thought of them as examples of poor planning.

As the months wore on from March, April, May and into June, 1934 an insidious enemy was robbing Byrd of all his strength--carbon monoxide

---

14 See Richard E. Byrd, 1938 *Alone* New York: G. P. Putnam's Sons.

poisoning from his gas stove. Eventually, his communications became so erratic that crew members like Waite and others grew alarmed and ventured forth in the dead of the Antarctic night to mount a rescue. They had to make three separate attempts to navigate south, losing trail flags to drifting snow, sledges and tractors falling into hidden crevasses, -75 degree blizzard temperatures and slipping clutches hampering their rescue attempts.

With each of us sipping hot coffee in *Glacier's* wardroom, Bud graphically described how cold it got on that rescue mission in 1934. "My hands, face and feet all got frostbitten. Thank God I didn't lose anything, but I accidentally touched a piece of frozen metal with my bare hand and lost a lot of flesh pulling it away. Ohhh! Godalmighty!" That was the sensation I had longed for as a thirteen year old, but hearing about its actuality from Bud sent shivers through my groin as we sat across from each other at the wardroom table with green felt table covering. I looked at his fingers to confirm that he still had his finger prints and he did.

"Generators going haywire, ignition failing every few minutes," he had told Little America on 10 August, 1934 during their third rescue mission. Looking at his weathered hands I tried to imagine them fussing with ignition wires at -50 in the Valley of Crevasses. How could you mess with thin wires while wearing thick woolen mittens? "You didn't," he said holding up his deeply scared fingers indicating that you had to remove your mittens to work on the engine. I knew then that my hands would have frozen and become worthless appendages.

Gulping his coffee like a veteran of so many polar voyages, Bud remembered the strange phenomenon of watching the "Now you see it, now you don't" lights on the horizon on his rescue mission.

"We saw one faint light on the horizon and then it disappeared, but we steered for it anyway. And then we saw it again and again it disappeared, as if we were rolling over depressions in the Barrier. Know what it was?" He was quizzing me the way my grandfather had with, "Why is the sun larger on the horizon than at its zenith?"

I thought for a second or two then replied, "Seeing Byrd's beacons through some kind of Barrier haze?" Sounded reasonable.

Nope! He grinned knowingly.

"Stars."

What?

"We were following the stars, or rather one in particular and we were veering off course to the east." My grandfather would have taken another step: trying to get me to visualize the earth rotating from west to east such that stars seemed down near the south pole to precess eastward and northward.

Bud remembered seeing green and red flares that Byrd later described as rags burning from a kite. Eventually they saw Byrd sitting in his brown fuzzy coat on a board between a couple of pieces of stove pipe. Bud rushed up to his commanding officer, whom he often referred to as "Skipper" or "the Admiral," and said, "How are you, Admiral?"

Byrd replied, "Come on below fellows, I have some hot soup waiting for you."[15]

When the three weary but relieved travelers followed Byrd down the trap door that had almost cost Byrd his life earlier, they came upon an almost unbelievable scene: a "litter of cans under the bunk" that told the story of their leader's slowly losing control of those faculties that mean survival in the world's most hostile environment. Bud radioed Little America: "Confidential. Found him weak from fumes."

Sitting in comfortable wardroom arm chairs with a tv mounted on the bulkhead, a stereo system playing a Johnny Cash song and drinking very hot, black coffee it was hard to imagine being so weak that keeping a flare burning for days and keeping soup hot on the stove would sap almost all of one's remaining strength.

Bud returned to telling me about the radio towers he helped construct, towers that beaconed the world about the community of explorers living on the dangerous ice barrier. In 1955 there were only a few feet remaining above the surface of the ice shelf. All else was crushed below the tons and tons of accumulated snow flakes, too many quadrillions to imagine.

"You were aboard *Glacier* then, with Byrd?"

"Yup, the maiden voyage of this old boat."

Amazing.

Above one of the radio beacons was his generator propeller which he then removed as a souvenir. "I felt I deserved to have it," he said with the

---

15 Bud Waite Letter to REB, 8/1938, Box 178/14, Byrd Archives, Ohio State University.

gleam of fond memory in his dark eyes. Nothing remained of his earlier homes but these three steel pinnacles jutting at a don Quixote tilt above the Barrier surface, nothing remained of his previous homes, nothing except the memory of laboring to establish the community, building the relationships amongst men who live, work and relax after a mission accomplished.

Bud reminds me so much of my grandfather who, according to his daughter, Anne, as a young boy self-taught himself all about electricity by taking books out of the library. Then with three buddies he erected wires stretching for about a mile from one house to another so they could communicate with one another, I presume by Morse Code. But Bud would have known what they evidently did not at such a tender age: that stringing such wires around high tension electrical cables could have fried them--

ZAP!--

in an instant.

Bud's stories romanced me back to the magic triangle. . ."Delicado's" harpsichord rhapsodized in the concert chambers of my mind as I remembered those days of trudging through Needham's snows searching for the coldest spot in Massachusetts,

imagining the bee sting of frost bite,

and snows so high you had to tunnel through to your own home. . .

Oh, the under-the-warm-covers-coziness of those tunnels!

When I told Bud about my own reasons for being onboard *Glacier*, about reading all those books, he suddenly startled me by saying almost casually, offhandedly,

"Byrd didn't write those books."

"What!" I sat up immediately realizing the fantasy had been assaulted, the pristine image of the hero had just suffered a sneak attack from a trustworthy witness to the truth.

"Murphy wrote those books."

What? Byrd didn't write the books that sent me down here?

Why is his name on them?

I said none of this to Bud, because the weight of his words did not sink in until later.

CJV Murphy was an executive assistant who in photographs is seen working at a typewriter and his name is given as author of two chapters of the story of the second expedition (*Discovery*, 1935) when Byrd was out at Advance Base. While reading these chapters years before, I had never noticed any real difference in tone or style, and now Bud was telling me that Murphy had authored both books.

Murphy wrote those books? with Byrd's name embossed in gold on the blue cover. Blue and gold, Navy colors.

What else was a lie?

The polar flight?

Discoveries in Marie Byrd Land?

Those footprints across the glistening snow toward the magic triangle?

What was hidden beneath those snows, in the tunnels, in the little workspaces where the pictures showed men smiling so perfectly into the Paramount movie cameras?

I sought no explanation, then.

Ask no questions. Were my grandfather sitting beside me he would have had so many curiosities. Why? How? When? What if. . ?

Were my mother sitting there at the table she would have asked Bud, "Well, how do you know Byrd didn't write them?"

I accepted what he said.

Why didn't I knock on this wardroom door either? Why didn't I press Bud about his statement just blurted out as if it were as evident as the emptiness of our coffee mugs?

I didn't really want to know.

I didn't want to violate the fantasy that had governed my life for more than a decade. Let the image created by that adolescent yearning for a hero amidst the litter of brown bottles around his house, let that picture shine ever so brightly in his consciousness.

But Bud Waite had planted the seed of doubt that lingered until my mother later brought it into full bloom.

>   Let "Delicado" continue her romantic rhapsody
>   Maybe it's not a lie
> Maybe a ghost writer
>   Don't disturb the fantasy
>   Ask no questions.
> Be marginal.
> Let the triangle be magical

15. Pete Demas, Dr. Thomas Poulter and Bud Waite depart for third time for Advance Base, August, 1934 with temperatures at -75.

Chapter Nine
The uniqueness of snowflakes

My mother often recalled talking to her father about snow flakes when she was still in high school in LeRoy, New York.

"Well, I don't believe it," she said so matter-of-factly that he must have wondered where he had gone wrong in raising her.

"What do you mean?" my grandfather said in some disbelief.

His daughter, then fifteen years old, was confronting him in the sun room of their large colonial home as snow gently began to cover the lawns of all the homes this Sunday afternoon.

"It just doesn't seem possible to me that all the snowflakes in the world--all those out there", she gestured with an exuberant sweep of her hand toward their front yard--"all those snow flakes are unique, that's all." She was calm.

The scientist, however, was becoming exasperated at his daughter's disbelief. "It's like finger prints, Betty. They're all different!"

"Well, I don't believe it! Do you mean that all the snowflakes out there--and all those all over New York are different from each other?"

"Yes," he said with the certainty of the scientist who had reasoned through the problem from knowledge of snow formation processes. It was as simple as that.

"And do you mean that they've all been different from the first one that ever fell on this country? I mean, how do you know?" Betty wasn't dazzled by her father's US Government patents for D-Zerta (first one in 1925)[16], a sugar-free gelatinous desert he had invented while working at the Jell-O division of General Foods Corporation. In the world of diabetics, L. Ray Ferguson would become a hero.

"Oh, you're impossible!" he said and with that he stormed out of the room leaving Betty to stare out the window and marvel at the descending evidence of Nature's wonders. There was the possibility of a school closing tomorrow on that blustery winter's day on East Main Street in LeRoy, not far from Rochester.

Elizabeth Lockwood Ferguson was very independent--a real daughter of that Republican who wanted to run over President Franklin Roosevelt while he was in his wheelchair. ("His New Deal is a raw deal for all of us!") She was intellectually tenacious and stubborn, and the apple of her father's eye, because she was such a good student. She got excellent grades, not because she was brilliant and didn't have to work hard, but because she was diligent and conscientious.

One of the most famous stories within our family, told by my grandfather, was that Betty had scored 100 on the New York State Geometry Regents examination. What a feat! Yes, indeed, she had an impressive talent for geometry and for taking tests, but not so commanding a presence that the secretaries at Wellesley College took notice.

My mother failed to attend Wellesley as a freshman, according to my grandfather, ". . .because, you know what? Those damned secretaries lost her application papers! Can you believe that?" I couldn't at the time I heard the story—when I was just applying to colleges myself.

They lost her papers! She scored 100 on the Geometry Regents and they couldn't find her papers, so she had to go somewhere else.

Mt. Holyoke--not a bad second choice.

---

16 Patent awarded to Llewellyn R. Ferguson of Le Roy, New York, 6 January, 1925. "The present invention relates to food product and the primary object is to provide a food product for diabetics or those suffering from other metabolic conditions in which carbohydrate[s] should be omitted. . . [consisting of] pure food gelatin. . .fruit acid. . . a carbohydrate-free sweetener. . .such as saccharin, dulcin or glucin." #1,522,428.

But Betty Ferguson thought the snowflakes couldn't all be unique, each and everyone markedly different from the other. How had she figured out that it was impossible for all the snowflakes falling in LeRoy on that stormy Sunday afternoon to be different?

Years later, I asked her. Just because there are so many, that's how. It wasn't difficult at all. My dad hadn't seen them all—no one has nor could see them all. Simple as that.

How many snowflakes could people have examined? Maybe a thousand or so, but think of the billions and billions of them out there that nobody has seen, she said mimicking astronomer Carl Sagan. "Billions and billions." How could you conclude from such a small sample size that each and every one of them was unique?

All our finger prints are unique.

But there aren't that many of us, compared with the snowflakes out there.

"I just didn't believe it and I still don't," she affirmed decades after her first pronouncement.

I guess my grandfather had figured it out differently.

What I never considered as a youngster hearing this story was how incisive my mother's reasoning was, how it challenged her father's thinking in ways I couldn't then imagine. She seemed naturally skeptical, perhaps learning that from her father in LeRoy.

"How do you know?" How does anybody know what she knows? What are the foundations of your conclusions? How can we be sure with such a limited sample? Betty Ferguson's imagination took her beyond what she could see in her front yard, beyond LeRoy to conceive of billions of unseen possibilities.

How can you be sure?

I had never thought of snow flakes as my mother did, and didn't conceive of their uniqueness when I was about to fly off to the South Pole. At last, after twelve years of dreaming and plotting, the Ultima Thule!

From that little closet on 23 Webster Park to the bottom of the world.

Imagine! Standing atop two miles of ice so tightly compacted that it took millions of years to accumulate and then millions more years to settle, allowing the bitterly cold winds to pack it down just as we used to do as kids breaking a path through the newly fallen snow out in the fields behind the school yard. Think of snow falling outside your window, flakes of all different shapes and sizes gently floating downward toward the ground. At first the ground is green with grass, but slowly it becomes white and after two days you have two feet of snow. Now think of the millions of flakes that have created these two feet: perhaps as many flakes as there are stars visible in the night sky. Then add to these stars those in the Milky Way multiplied by all the galaxies visible with the Mt. Palomar and Hubble Space telescopes. Then all of these nearly countless stars would be equivalent to the number of flakes required to bury your entire house after two weeks of snowfall.

Now imagine not just your house and its 30 foot height above ground, but all of the houses that make up a height of nine thousand five hundred feet--that is, about three hundred and sixteen houses standing atop each other and think of how many more particles of snow had to fall to cover them. All of the stars in the entire visible universe stretching out some 14 billion light years and then those visible only with all of the optical and radio telescopes on earth and multiply these billions and billions of stars by all of the drops of water in the Atlantic and Pacific Oceans and you might approximate the number of snow flakes that would fall in those several millions of years to create the south polar plateau.

I wish my grandfather were here now to help me imagine the infinitude of these flakes at the South Pole. He might be just as amazed as I am by the impossibility of one's mind to grasp the immensity of time's effect upon that one geographical spot on earth—the South Pole. How long it took to accumulate two miles of ice we do not know. Some speculate that it has taken the past fifteen million years.

What we do know is that Latitude 90 South—a fixed point on our global charts-- hasn't moved. The continent that now resides around the Pole, however, has been propelled by plate tectonics over hundreds of millions of years from places like present-day Texas and, subsequently, Australia.

Imagine standing on a surface once trod upon by Amundsen and Scott and beholding the vast plateau and its seemingly limitless horizon. You turn 360 degrees from the Pole and all directions are north--the only geographical point on earth where all directions are the same, save for the north pole. How Ray Ferguson loved to challenge all eleven of his grandchildren to imagine this geographical fact! (Only he used the North Pole.)

Here was a man-made reference point that is stationary on our charts, but the place marked on the continent as the bottom of the world or the "last spot of the world" as Shackleton called it is in continual motion. The spot where Amundsen pitched his tent in December, 1911 is several miles from where our C-130 would land, because the polar plateau is in continual motion, pressing toward the coast lines as if moving there to spawn those stately caravels we'd seen steaming through the Ross Sea.

Here was a spot where temperatures of -102 had been recorded by Paul Siple, the Eagle Scout with Byrd on all of his previous expeditions, as he established our first permanent outpost there in 1958. Here it took a steak one week to thaw out and a bonfire failed to melt any of the ice beneath your feet. Nevertheless, Siple was able to grow the first polar philodendron during his wintering over experience, a lovely and ranging green plant similar to the ones my mother nursed to full growth in all the homes we lived in.

Ever since reporting aboard *Glacier*, I had told my story not only to Captain Grant but to the Executive Officer Lt. Commander Swope.

"That would be a non-mission flight," he said. In the military there were regulation duties, and special operations in accordance with your group's mission. Sending Lt. John Barell to the South Pole was definitely not within the scope of being Operations Officer of *Glacier*. We couldn't break ice all the way to the Pole.

"Yes, sir, I know." But I proceeded to ply him with the story and added a few reasons while standing at his cabin door, across a brief passageway from my own in forward officer's country.

"It would provide *Glacier's* Public Information image with a boost—first Officer to stand at the Pole."

"Go on," he said with a slight smile taking another drag on his ever present cigarette.

"This trip would extend *Glacier's* glory farther than Hut Point—"

"We need that after all the dignitaries we've had aboard?" And he proceeded to rattle off names like Francis Cardinal Spellman of the New York Archdiocese, scientists like Van Allen and Admirals of the Fleet, including Byrd.

I added a few more reasons that made the "XO" just grin even wider as if he were hearing one of those "sea stories" told by a sailor who was late getting back off liberty.

"Oh, hell, Commander, I've dreamt of this for over ten years. I want to go because it's been a goal for all that time; because I want to write about it; because—"

"OK, Shut up, already," he said wanting to get back to the paper work on his desk. "I'll see what I can do."

With that I thanked him and day after day popped into his office or encountered him on the weather decks with a quizzical look in my eye.

"Just hang in there, buddy boy," he'd say.

Well, it didn't work out quite as I had planned. Wanting so much to stand at the South Pole I had prepared myself for the day when the Executive Officer would ask, Do you want to fly to the Pole? Only what he said was, We can't get to the Pole this trip. They have a flight going off to the Russian base somewhere. Are you interested?

Yes! But what a disappointment not to be flying the route of Scott and Amundsen and over the Queen Maud Mountains where Byrd had dumped a sack of food in 1929 and Dr. Gould had found samples of low grade coal. The South Pole was the bottom of the world, the spot Greek philosophers envisioned as a continent where all laws known to them were reversed. They called it "Antarctos," or "against the bear." The bear was *Ursa Major*, a constellation containing the Big Dipper that dominated the northern skies above Athens. My grandfather had taught me about the Dipper with its pointer stars leading to Polaris so long ago. You can always find your way home, he had said pointing northward, if you can find Polaris, the North Star.

My problem now was being smuggled aboard a US Navy C-130 transport flying from Williams Field, McMurdo Station to the Russian base, Vostok.

I knew next to nothing about Vostok except that it lay somewhere near the South Geomagnetic Pole and sat on a plateau some 11,000 feet high, making it higher than the Pole itself. It lay in the vicinity of what cartographers called the Point of Inaccessibility, the farthest geographical point in Antarctica from any ocean.

I showed up at Williams Field with all my cameras and as much foul weather gear on as I could manage plus a few candy bars from the stewards to ward against hunger on what would be a long flight. The C-130 aircraft stood ready for take-off at Williams Field, an ice runway built during Operation

Deep Freeze One. It was a giant black petrel of a bird revving its engines to keep all the fluids from freezing. I wondered if they ever used blow torches as Byrd did in 1929 before his historic flight.

Finally, the cargo bay door was closed and an airman stood in the middle of aircraft surrounded by those brown boxes marked "USARP" and counted heads. He counted twenty one and said to himself "There's only supposed to be twenty here." He started counting again and I knew I should say something. But if I did, I was afraid of being bumped even though there was plenty of room. "Should I say something?" Visions of so many "shoulds" paraded across my mental stage: "You should always be on time, do what you're told, eat spinach. . ." and on and on! He kept counting and scratching his head. This time he went forward to tell his bosses in the cockpit.

One of the pilots was the captain who had given me permission to fly, but I knew that the wing commander of the whole navy air detachment was riding along and he probably didn't know about my presence. What if the kid tells the old man and they ask, 'Who's the stowaway?' Then I'll have to stand up. Goddammit! Maybe I *should* go up there now and confess, as I did in Needham when the police car drove slowly down Webster Park to see who had set that old Christmas wreath on fire behind our neighbor's garage.

When the airman came back he no longer had the clipboard so I assumed I was safely aboard.

As we lifted off the icy Williams field runway I looked out the window like any young tourist. You could see more of the weather vane of smoke emanating from the crater of Erebus. The steamy, wispy column rising just a few hundred feet or so and then spreading out to the northwest contained none of the glow of red hot lava that others had noticed. In 1841 Ross and his men saw a great column of black smoke rising with red tinges of fire at the crater. In 1907 Shackleton and his men, camped on its volcanic shores at Cape Royds saw "great bursts of flame crowning the crater."[17]

When you look at a volcano such as Erebus you see it as a peaceful, snowy breast silhouetted against the deep blue Antarctic sky. All active volcanoes are the surface expression of earth's deep molten turbulence. No one, however,

---

17   E. H. Shackleton 1909. *The Heart of the Antarctic—Being the story of the British Antarctic Expedition 1907-1909*. Philadelphia: J. B. Lippincott Company p. 172.

has ever reported fiery lava rising over the crater's lip and melting down the sleek slopes of this volcano.

From my height of a few thousand feet as we banked first toward the south and then westward, I wondered about the crater. Or I should say, the fourth crater, for Erebus actually is composed of four superimposed craters. Shackleton noted that as you climb toward the summit you encounter one crater at 6000 feet that is about six miles in diameter and on up toward the summit there are two more with the final one composed "chiefly of fragments of pumice." [18] How and when did these other craters form? How old was Antarctica herself when Erebus began to rear her volcanic head above the snows? Or was there even snow on her surface as she moved inch by inch over the earth's surface in her inexorable march south to her current resting place? Where had she been when Erebus was born? In Gondwanaland some 65 millions years ago, closer to the Roaring Forties?

Time's slow dance across the face of the planet was here evident on the slopes of Erebus.

And as I flew over this outpouring of subterranean power, I knew my father would have loved being in the bucket seat right next to me. He would have reveled in the plane's response to turbulence above Erebus. He once told me about something called "an air pocket," where flying along on a clear day you'd hit a vacuum in the sky and drop thousands of feet!

He loved riding his DC-3s perhaps hoping for a sudden drop of a thousand feet.

But the bouncing around made me nervous and I held on to the straps of the bucket seat with a firm grip.

More than the rattling of the fuselage, he would have enjoyed his first sightings--of Erebus, the Prince Albert Range of mountains and the polar plateau. He probably would have regaled me, over the roar of the engines sucking up the rarefied polar air, with stories of his first flights over the Rocky Mountains and how insignificant he felt in their monumental presence.

"We are like flies on the face of the highest mountains, John," he once wrote me. He saw our presence in the world as did landscape painters like Jacob von Ruysdale, Thomas Cole, Frederick Church and those from Asia—

---

18   Shackleton, p. 193.

human beings dwarfed by the magnificence, power and towering beauty of nature.

How he would have loved all this, pressing his nose against the windows gazing down upon Nature's mantle of power folding up through the deep glacial crusts. He daydreamed of things unseen, like his beloved computer reservation project.

It was George Bernard Shaw who said,

> *Some men see things as they are and ask*
> *why. Others dream things that never were and ask why not.*

That was my father.

We set course right over Mt. Lister and sped our way toward the great western plateau and probably passed directly over the spot where Scott had his farthest westing in 1903. Now I, like Captain Robert Falcon Scott, was off toward the unknown, a word that still rings with the mystery he recorded back in his little green tent atop the Ferrar Glacier.

I recalled my own search for the unknown-- Perhaps any one of these mountains was the size of Mt. Grace McKinley in Marie Byrd Land, the peak I wanted to own part of not too many years ago. Named after the wife of Byrd's photographer and third in command in 1928, this "mountain" was only about 2,000 feet above the snows to the east of Little America.

I had written the Secretary of the Interior, a man by the name of Chapman, asking if I could

> *. . .purchase a few acres of land at the base of Mt. Grace McKinley in Marie Byrd Land at approximately latitude 77 degrees 56 minutes South and longitude 148 degrees 10 minutes West. . .I am interested in the governmental regulations concerning the possibility of this purchase.*

What I wanted then was a little corner of the world all my own. Our home on 23 Webster Park now had little Robin gurgling, crying and waking up at all hours of the night for mother to breast feed her. I had my little closet for clothes and reading, but what boy of thirteen doesn't want a hiding place, a place of his own to make into a little palace? I'd built caves out of snow drifts and they were what I imagined I'd have in Marie Byrd Land, a place all of my own where no sisters would wander and my father and his loud protestations of being "an idea man, not a 9 to 5 worker" would be thousands of miles away. Some little acreage of snow and ice with my name on it. Seemed like a reasonable request.

I had no plan then for making a down payment on the land. Perhaps I would have used my allowance, or gone out to sell newspapers or Christmas wreaths as my Uncle Ken helped me do that winter.

And, come to think of it, I wasn't sure how I would gain access to my little corner of the world. I'd solve that problem when I was able to follow Admiral Byrd, perhaps sail with him down south.

Unfortunately, no one from the Interior Department found my request worth answering so I didn't have to worry about high financing at this early age. I imagined them puzzled by this request to purchase land, perhaps laughing it off or just filing it away under "Miscellaneous."

I settled in for a long flight over a vast featureless expanse of ice, nothing below to mark any geological activity, nothing to navigate from, nothing to aid in your journeys from home. I wondered if the pilots were using a bubble sextant to shoot the sun, a device Byrd pioneered in creating and using on his own flight to the South Pole in 1929.

Erebus was well over the horizon, but still on my mind. That lofty beacon so softly rounded at the top and my father were too much alike, so seemingly quiet and composed. But both grew over time through several different personas, different false faces presented to the world. And deep within each were these simmering cauldrons of raw energy that spilled out in public for all to see. Deep subterranean forces keep the fiery magma in a molten state-- forever recasting, refashioning the faces of Nature.

So it was with my father, and I wondered how mother, Missy and Little Robin were coping with his passionate eruptions.

Were he and Robin, who was now thirteen, playing Rummy in front of the fire place? And was Little Robin up to her tricks, beating him at the game he had taught all of us?

"What? How did you *do* that, you little monkey?"

She had won. She won consistently and this drove him to exasperation. He couldn't understand how this little seventh grader could beat the master at Rummy.

"We'll play again!"

Again she beat him.

"Oh, my god!" Again the red hand slapped his forehead in disbelief. "What are you doing to me? This is terrible!" He had probably had one or two drinks, but this didn't keep Robin from working her strategy.

She was cheating.

Yes, Little Robin, the baby with the soft spot just above her forehead when this whole adventure began (in 1951) had grown up into a smart little girl who could outwit her father.

"Shoot! This is unbelievable!" He couldn't accept that he, of all people, the master of RESERVATRON had been beaten by a thirteen year old.

But she cheated well. She sat there cross legged holding her cards close but reading his cards, spade for spade, heart for heart in the reflection of his thick glasses. Badly nearsighted, but not in his own mind.

He never caught on and kept on losing.

" What are you doing to me?" He leaned back completely mystified by his younger daughter's mastery of the game. She outsmarted him at his own game of hearts, because she had learned something Antarctica demands as well: wits. Not only did you need determination; you also needed the wits to out think your opponent. You needed a strategy, a plan.

Little Robin had a plan. She knew what she was about.

16. *Winging past Erebus enroute Vostok*

Chapter Ten
Vostok—near the Point of Inaccessibility

We landed after a three hour flight even more bumpily than we took off and once again I was amazed and ever conscious of the advances in polar travel since 1912. The aircraft cabin wasn't heated too well, but at least it wasn't -60 inside and we were always above the storms and the soft snows that Scott and his men had endured back at the turn of the century.

I stepped out onto the polar plateau at an elevation of over 11,000 feet above sea level. The ice beneath my feet was two miles thick all the way down to the bottom where the land was about 1,000 feet below sea level, perhaps sunk beneath sea-level with the weight of all that ice.

The C-130 sat like a giant green spider perched atop the snow plateau threatening any intruder with the ear shattering noise of her engines kept running against the -25 degree cold.

Momentarily, I stood in the middle of a vast desert, where very little snow falls at all, seeing nothing out to the horizon for 360 degrees, nothing to break the monotony of ice and what the Russians had so long ago called "sastrugi," those icy waves in the snow that made sled travel so miserable. My father would have looked out upon this landscape and seen a symphony of rhythmic cadences in these snowy breakers blown out across the plateau. He was always thinking mathematically, seeing numbers and patterns in Beethoven's symphonies as well as in his balance sheets.

I felt alone but wonderfully at home. Here was the center of all those closet dreams only twelve years ago, dreams of being a polar explorer alongside Byrd. But now I was standing under a cloudless blue sky with the snow almost blinding me. Watch out for snow blindness. I had wanted to suffer frostbite, but never snow blindness.

Alone and excited, I wanted to run off in all directions just to explore, to get away from this tiny community of Russian scientists and experience the Antarctic desert, to be trudging off across the sastrugi to make a discovery, to camp out with the "fellows" and pull our sleds toward the horizon. But now I had "to hit the head" after such a long flight without using any bathroom facilities. I had never thought about peeing in the desert! The Russians had to have an outhouse indoors.

Whereas McMurdo Station sat on jet black volcanic residue, Vostok was set into the polar plateau just as Little America had been at the Bay of Whales. I was immediately surprised by the brilliant reds of some of the exposed buildings, expecting I guess that all of them would have been deeply buried by now.

In 1928 you entered Little America from a hatch or igloo-like opening near one of the main buildings; here at Vostok you walked down a gentle slope toward an exposed door and into a passageway that led into what appeared to be a main meeting and dining area. Just as in Byrd's day, rooms served multiple purposes to conserve space and this one had a few men in khaki sweaters, and red suspenders hovering around a chart on a folding table. I wasn't exactly sure of what to do or where to go. I considered approaching these fellows speaking Russian, but decided against it, since they seemed too intent on figuring something out.

I looked for the underground passageways lined above with crates of frozen foodstuffs as in Little America. I wanted to run my hands over those boxes and imagine the weight of snow above them. I wanted to see the tunnel doors full of ice crystals so thick that when you brushed by one a cascading rain of ice fell down your neck and almost froze you in your tracks. But Vostok wasn't like the Little America of the 1920's and 30's. No, it was more like walking through a scientific laboratory anywhere in a remote outpost. The passageways were more like those on *Glacier*--neat, clean and with much of the bulkhead space covered with photos of resident scientists and charts of various kinds.

And no one looked at all menacing. These Russian scientists did not appear to have their fingers on any intercontinental ballistic missiles. They did not look like Khrushchev ready to go to war over missiles in Cuba. They did not reflect the possibility of international terror Kennedy had spoken of. The Russians looked just like the men on Byrd's expeditions, sporting long dark beards just as I imagined characters in Dostoevsky's *Crime and Punishment* or *Brothers Karamazov*. They looked like Dmitri and Ivan Karamazov or maybe even a young Raskolnikov without the evil intentions.

Deep within the interior spaces of this base run by our cold war adversaries, I found a very engaging glaciologist who, after pointing to the head, explained the nature of his work to me. I could converse in his native language upon graduation from Harvard, but now I struggled to understand his explanations of drilling down through the ice to retrieve cores that tell the story of our atmosphere 1, 2 and 300,000 years ago. . .about the cores. . .about oxygen content. . . about the ages of the ice. . .What was the word for "one hundred thousand?"

He spoke rather slowly, but I kept asking him with much embarrassment to repeat. ("Ya nee panyeemayoo.") Most of the time I just nodded as he pointed to the chart and then to a model of an ice core. Once he wrote out some atmospheric formulas on a pad of paper that suggested life on earth many years ago was very different. Not so much carbon dioxide in the air, he said. Pollution now, he said.

What they were studying, life on earth as revealed in the ice cores, was never anything I'd ever thought of. Perhaps my grandfather had, but now I was struggling with the language to understand how the atmospheric conditions of the world, as revealed in these tiny bubbles, had changed at different stages in their several hundred thousand year history.

From his demonstrations and drawings I was able to understand that the Russians were drilling down through the polar ice cap with a hollow tube that extracts an ice core from as deep as 11,000 feet down. Each layer of the core represented a season of snow fall and whatever was part of the precipitation: including wind-blown dust, ash, atmospheric gases, even radioactivity. From these cores we can infer the impact of the accumulation of "greenhouse gases" like carbon dioxide and make predictions about their impact in the future. One core dated back to 160,000 years ago and showed seasons of global warming and high levels of these gases. But back then there was no one burning "fossil fuels," so where did all the carbon dioxide and methane come from?

Perhaps the heating of the planet we thought we were experiencing was the result of natural earth dynamics?

I got so engrossed in listening to and trying to interpret my teacher's assessment of their scientific program that I hardly heard the shouting until it was almost in my face: Where is that sailor?

Now, they're after me, I thought.

Then he appeared in the doorway. "Hey! You're supposed to be on that goddamned plane!" He turned around assuming I would follow immediately.

And I did. I bowed and thanked my host ("spacebo bolshoi") for his time with some kind of hurried phrase that probably translated to "I'm so glad I will be your friend in the near future."

I ran down the corridors trying not to smash my cameras into the bulkheads, crashed into one mole of a person creeping out of his room. "Pardon!" I said in English.

I got out of the main door and started running straight ahead, head down as if I were running with the football through the Yale line with all my cumbersome foul weather gear. I heard nothing besides the roar of the engines and didn't think of the co-pilot, my benefactor on this flight, keeping the plane on the ground long enough to make sure I got home to McMurdo. What if they had taken off? I would probably be stranded here for days, perhaps weeks. I would have been "AWOL," absent without leave. Bad record. . .no career in the Navy, but it probably would have stayed with me through whichever graduate school I chose--the black sheep of the Navy. "Boy most likely to succeed" missing in Antarctica! No future for you. You get a B in math and physics, a friend had said, and you can forget the Ivy League! Oh, my god.

"Hey! You crazy bastard! Watch where you're goin!"

I was running head down toward the sound and would have run right under the wing and into the whirring and revving port props. And that would have been the end of flight #786 from McMurdo to Vostok and back and the end of a short and rather exciting sojourn in Antarctica for one young naval officer. Untimely ripped asunder by the churning Pratt & Whitney engines kept roaring in the -25 degree temperatures, I would have been strewn in several bloody parts onto the south polar plateau 12,200 feet above the single celled creatures that might exist so far below.

I skidded a foot over the iron-crusted polar plateau, stood bolt upright, saw the blurry black props chopping through the polar air, shuddered heavily and re-directed myself toward the aft hatch. I found a bucket seat and spread out, since there was a lot more room on the return flight. We had left a lot of brown boxes at Vostok and a few passengers. I saw no one who looked noticeably Russian making this flight to McMurdo. As we taxied down the even bumpier ice way, I knew the co-pilot must be regretting the moment he said to my Executive Officer, "Sure! Why not? Anything for a shipmate!" Shipmates are one thing, but shipmates of shipmates are quite another matter. They would have been justified in taking off without me, but he stayed and I wondered what I should say to him later on, if anything.

We lifted off and I peered out the small window to watch Vostok grow smaller and the redness of one of its prominent buildings dim in the glare of the sun's fading rays off the ice cap. I kept thinking about what the scientist had said about pollution in the ice, carbon dioxide, trapped in little bubbles.

Their drilling down thousands of feet below the surface "sastrugi" was science, amazingly original and pristine, just like Cherry-Garrard's and Wilson's pursuit of penguin teeth and a possible link to dinosaurs. Both Russians and Englishmen asked tough questions of Nature and pursued truth back to more than 420 million years ago. The search for details of bubbles and teeth could sweep away the falsity of untested assumptions, the numbness of vague abstractions and glittering generalities that covered our ignorance.[19]

We sped east toward McMurdo, Erebus and the company of shipmates on *Glacier*.

---

19 Recently a report from the Intergovernmental Panel on Climate Change said "the likelihood was 90 percent to 99 percent that emissions of heat-trapping greenhouse gases like carbon dioxide, spewed from tailpipes and smokestacks, were the dominant cause of the observed warming of the last 50 years. In the panel's parlance, this level of certainty is labeled 'very likely.'" Dr. Susan Soloman, senior scientist at NOAA, has spearheaded coordinating the work of IPCC. *The New York Times*, February 6, 2007. p. F3.

Chapter Eleven
Grains of Sand like the Gobi Desert

It was February 25 and the earth was inexorably tilting away from the sun in these southern regions precessing on it axis and darkness would enshroud first McMurdo, then Vostok and, finally, the Pole Station.

As we sped homeward I kept peering out the windows waiting for our first sighting of the Transantarctic Mountains, that chain of peaks running from Cape Adare up north to within several hundred miles of the Pole itself. There was the Beardmore Glacier, that massive highway first sighted by Shackleton in 1908 on his attempt to reach the furthest south. I wanted so much to fly low over that great river of frozen power, to find what Shackleton called "The Cloud Maker," a mountain with clouds resting atop its peak, to see where Scott rested in 1912 for a lunch en route home from the Pole, having lost the race to Amundsen by four weeks, where Dr. Wilson would have gone rock hunting and found "*Glossopteris*," the fossil fern from millions of years ago.

I had written one of Scott's geologists, Frank Debenham, asking him about Scott and he replied from England that Scott was a fine leader, one who would, however, be down on a man "like a shot" if he detected anything like "prevarication."

"What does 'prevarication' mean?" I asked my mother.

"It's a lie, an untruth," she said as she admired the fineness of Debenham's handwriting, small and precise lettering befitting a renowned scientist.

Debenham had researched the Beardmore region and concluded that it was once below water and now held "beds of black limestone containing fossils of corals."

Corals. Which tropical blue waters had spawned these little creatures and when were they deposited on the slopes of what we now call the Beardmore Glacier?

He also investigated the Royal Society Range opposite his hut at Cape Evans and noted that on these precipitous slopes there were "grains of sand [that] are very well rounded, as though wind worn. . .and there are remains of fresh-water plants in these bands."

> *From those facts we can postulate a low-lying area with sand-dunes or desert sand in the neighbourhood, which was collected and redeposited, probably by water. . . For this period, therefore, we may not be far wrong if we imagine a land somewhat approaching in conditions the Southern Sahara or the outskirts of the Gobi Desert. Too much emphasis must not be laid upon its desert character, however, for our only evidence for that is the wind-blown appearance of the sand grains, and the absence of fossils in the sandstone itself.*[20]

But Debenham reserved his highest praise for the geologizing done by Dr. Wilson and "Birdy Bowers" en route from the Pole to their home at Cape Evans, McMurdo Sound.

> *The plant fossils collected by this party are the best preserved of any yet found in this quadrant of the Antarctic and are of the character best suited to settle a long-standing controversy between geologists as to the nature of the former union between Antarctica and Australasia."* [21]

---

20 Frank Debenham, 1913 "The Geological History of South Victoria Land," in *Scott's Last Expedition*, Volume II, New York: Dodd, Mead and Company, pp 295-300.
21 Frank Debenham, 1913, "Summary of Geological Journeys," in *Scott's Last Expedition*, Volume II. New York: Dood, Mead and Company, p. 302.

So, Frank Debenham, who responded so promptly to the query of a wondering fourteen year old American lad, was suggesting what Alfred Wegener had proposed during the same year, 1912, that the earth's continents were once joined, that Antarctica may have been contiguous with Australia. Wegener proposed a theory of "continental drift" hypothesizing that each continent sat atop a plate of earth's crust and that over millions of years these plates had been ever so slowly moving and colliding with each other. He pointed to the way Africa and South America seemed like puzzle pieces fitting together rather neatly. The only missing element in his theory was just what propelled these continents away from each other.

Wegener was ridiculed by fellow geologists (not Debenham, I assume) but eventually the discovery of similar plants and animals, including dinosaurs (*Cryolophosaurus*) and reptiles (*Lystrosaurus*) in Antarctica, Australia, and Africa seems to confirm this contention. Antarctica has not always been alone, isolated, subducted into an icy and wild existence.

Like Cherry-Garrard and other men on Scott's last expedition, Debenham traveled not for the glory of being number one, but to learn about this most remote continent on the planet. "We traveled for science." To add to the world's knowledge, to stand firm on data and not rely on myth and assumption.

Just like my grandfather, scientist Llewellyn Ray Ferguson who had created D-Zerta, the gelatinous desert for diabetics.

Men who teach us the value of considering the data--look to the grains of sand, the fossils of *Glossopteris* and *Cryolophosaurus*. Don't let myth, magic and mystery gain the upper hand of our thinking. Consider what's in front of you; ask what it relates to before drawing conclusions.

For Debenham it was grains of sand, not too unlike those contemplated by poet William Blake:

> *To see a World in a Grain of Sand,*
> *And a Heaven in a Wild Flower,*
> *Hold Infinity in the palm of your hand,*
> *And Eternity in an hour.* ("Auguries of Innocence," 1800-1810)

As we began our descent I know we passed so close to the last resting place of Scott and his men, where, within 11 miles of One Ton Depot, Scott, Wilson and "Birdie" Bowers expired within their green tent in 1912 slowly being buried by hurricane winds that prevented their moving toward home. Good old Titus Oates' body lay somewhere down there.

"I'm just going out and I may be some time," Oates had said crawling out to his death as the British explorers suffered from unusually brutal storms. As I flew over their grave sight I had no idea that some rescuers speculated that they had died of the sailor's most dreaded disease, scurvy.

Under Scott's leadership, they had made some fatal errors. Their diet was insufficiently full of fat that produced calories. When they needed 6,000 calories, according to Cherry-Garrard, they had almost one third of that.

When they had planned for four men to leg it to the Pole, Scott at the last minute added a fifth.

They had poor navigational equipment, according to one source.

And they refused to take and kill dogs along the way, as Amundsen had done.

Make your plan and work your plan, my father said.

They have to be good, reasonable plans first.

But a more recent and incisive analysis by Dr. Susan Solomon[22] concluded that all of these challenges could have been overcome had Scott not suffered the worst weather conditions on the Great Ross Ice Shelf. He experienced what she called "The Coldest March" on record. Solomon noted that terrible blizzards dealt Scott an unseasonably "crushing blow" leaving them "exceedingly unlucky," and leading to their deaths. Again, we confront the facts Wilson and Cherry-Garrard sought with those three Cape Crozier embryos and discover new truths: "a little more knowledge, that [the world] may build on what it knows instead of on what it thinks."

We veered to port on our approach to Williams Field bringing Mt. Erebus into view once again. A thick column of white smoke rose into the

---

22 Solomon, Susan. 2001. *The Coldest March—Scott's Fatal Antarctic Expedition.* New Haven: Yale University Press. "I will show that in the last month of their lives, nature dealt them a crushing blow in the form of conditions that can now be shown to be far colder than normal, and therefore radically different from those they quite sensibly expected to find. In simple terms, Scott and his men did everything right regarding the weather but were exceedingly unlucky." P. xvii.

deep Antarctic blueness from its deep cauldrons, looking like the mushroom cloud over Hiroshima.

The next day we set sail from McMurdo for the last time. All the bay ice had been broken and blown northward out into the Ross Sea. We were moored alongside Hut Point where Scott's first hut still stood, full of snow blown through worn fittings and openings. It stood near our mooring beneath the cross erected by Cherry-Garrard for Scott and his four companions who never made it home from the South Pole, an adventure gone terribly awry. The inscription, from Tennyson's "Ulysses," read "to strive, to seek, to find and not to yield."

After clearing our mooring we steamed northeastward, past Cape Evans where I raised a hand in salute to Scott and his men.

Later that afternoon, with sea smoke forming over the waters of McMurdo in late March foretelling the onset of the polar winter, our radio operators patched in a call home through a ham radio operator in Connecticut. I wanted to tell my folks that the adventure was coming to a close. But the atmospheric conditions across the nine thousand miles were not very good.

"fine. . . over. . .

. . . being national consultant. . . ov. . .

Say again. . .Over. . ."

I managed to figure out through the static of the ionosphere's bouncing our signal up and down across the earth, that my father had been drinking before our conversation and I worried about mother, Missy and Robin.

How were they coping?

It was many years later that mother told me that the inevitable had happened.

He'd been fired. His boss, Mr. Kelsey, had had enough of his coming to work slightly inebriated.

All the dirty brown bottles with little white seals around the neck had finally dashed his transcending imagination and left him with no chart on which to make his mark.

My father soon started his wandering over the face of the earth in search of a new self just as Antarctica had been doing for over seven hundred million years.

Antarctica was not what it seemed and neither were her heroes.

With my mother's help I would find all of this out soon enough.

17. Royal Society Range where Frank Debenham, found "sand grains" similar to those of Gobi Desert.

18. The loneliness of long distance travelers

Part II: New Horizons

Chapter Twelve
Running aground

There was a brass plate just on the bridge of one ship I sailed on reading, "A collision at sea can ruin your whole day."

Indeed!

But a fate equally as horrible could be that of running your ship aground in uncharted waters.

My very first captain was Hart Dale Hilton, an aviator who had flown with Admiral Halsey in the Pacific and had suffered as a Japanese prisoner of war from 1942-1945. No stranger to adversity, Captain Hilton knew how to plan, how to execute and how to be very mindful of danger.

On a sunny August 1960 day onboard *Mauna Kea* (AE-22) Captain Hilton was watching the pilot navigate his ship up the murky waters of the Sacramento River north of San Francisco en route to our berth at Port Chicago, where all of the ammunition ships tied up. This was far enough away from Oakland and San Francisco in case there were an explosion similar to the one in 1944 at this depot that killed so many sailors and dock handlers.

I was on the flying bridge, the highest deck on the ship from which we could navigate up river. I had been on board only a few weeks and was just getting comfortable using binoculars and being the best lookout that I could. Only a few weeks previous I had marched through Harvard Yard to "Pomp and Circumstance" trying to catch a glimpse of the tall, auburned hair presidential candidate, Senator John F. Kennedy, marching at his alma mater during the ceremonies.

All of a sudden Captain Hilton yelled, *"Let go the port anchor! All back emergency."*

The telephone talker barked these commands into his sound-powered phones that relayed them up to the special sea and anchor detail on the bow. I heard the commotion of the boatswain's mate taking sledge hammer to the clip holding the port anchor on deck. It crackled down into the muddy waters through the hawse hole just as the engines began to rumble in reverse. I looked over the port wing of the bridge where the Captain and the pilot were standing and felt the ship ever so slowly gain sternway.

I looked at the other junior officer and asked what had happened.

"I dunno," he said.

The captain later explained that he felt the bow of the ship "touch bottom" and he acted to prevent any structural damage. Subsequently, he ordered a diver to inspect the ship's bow beneath the water line and, as everybody suspected, they found no damage.

"You've got to think and act quickly, taking all precautions," he said later in a moment of reflection. Captain Hart Dale Hilton was a model of prudent leadership, ensuring that all details were considered and nothing was overlooked. Four years later I recalled his actions as we neared the end of our polar journey.

After sailing thousands of miles through uncharted Antarctic waters, we came perilously close to a major catastrophe that would have ruined not just my day at sea.

I was at the conn following our navigator's plot en route to McMurdo near one of the more majestic islands, Beaufort Island, just ten miles north of our destination. Here was a subterranean mountain rising above the ocean floor, presenting to the navigator her sheer black cliffs rising 1,600 feet above the eastern waterline, while the western coast gave us a long ice slope terminating at the sea. Volcanic in origin, the island was named after Sir Francis Beaufort of the Royal Navy. We regularly used the Beaufort Scale to register the force of the wind—0 being very light air and 12 being a full hurricane.

As we steamed along on this cloudy afternoon, I started hearing the fathometer ping with what Byrd had called "ever increasing acceleration."

It became more frequent meaning that we were pinging bottom sooner—-it was getting shallower. I ignored it for a while, keeping to the navigator's track because I assumed he knew what he was doing.

Then all of a sudden I became very nervous as the pinging became louder and even more frequent. *Glacier* drew 28 feet and the rocky foothills of Beaufort were drawing nigh faster and faster.

Suddenly I looked at the fathometer and saw there was only 100 feet beneath the keel.

Holy shit!

"Right Full Rudder! All ahead Full!" I ordered.

"Call the Captain!"

The bosun piped over the 1MC, the ship's internal communications medium, "Now, Captain, Please come to the bridge!"

When members of ship's company hear that announcement, hearts skip a beat wondering what terrible event has happened? What danger has the Officer of the Deck gotten us into?

Captain Vaughan came racing up to the bridge. I explained the situation, nervous about his response. But he accepted my actions as appropriate and asked to be kept advised of any future submersibles menacing the ship.

We steamed out of there safely and I'll never forget that I almost put the ship up onto the rocks, berthing her on an under-the-sea foothills of Beaufort Island. Everything looked so placid, so quiet, except for the ever present pinging on the bridge! I had almost ignored those danger signals and the deep sea realities hidden beneath a calm, placid surface.

For years thereafter I recalled this near grounding and the full collision at sea on my previous ship when we ignominiously slammed into the starboard aircraft elevator of USS *Kearsarge*. I still remember the fact that I took sufficient action to avert disaster in the one case and suffered the ignominy of a lousy, unfair, biased and re-thinking-of-history-fitness report in the other.

But an equally apprehensive experience came in teaching a group of ninth graders that first semester in New York City. The Navy was interested in my ability to speak Russian and wanted me to attend foreign language school at Monterey. I had thought that maybe working for United Press International in Europe would be exciting and even had an interview with a CIA agent who assured me that Agency men sleuthing about in dark trench coats was a stereotype.

I decided not to use my facility with the Russian language to spy on the Soviet Union sitting at a console all day somewhere in Germany translating pages and pages of encoded messages.

Like so many of my contemporaries I had been inspired by President Kennedy's creation of the Peace Corps and had earned a slot teaching in Kenya, but thought that working with kids in New York City was the kind of domestic corps I wanted to belong to just then.

I decided that my heart lay with my own mentors, Claire Slattery and Wilbury Crockett and became an English teacher at Charles Evans Hughes High School on west 18th street in Manhattan. They gave me five classes of students right off the bat without any practice teaching. The department chair looked forward to having a former naval officer with a firm handshake in the classroom, the hallways and the lunch room.

Teaching in New York City seemed far removed from fleet operations in the Pacific and in the Ross Sea. Here my challenge was to get students as engaged as possible in writing, reading and thinking about the issues of life. I knew that Slattery and Crockett had asked me to do more than memorize text. They insisted that I use my mind to analyze literature and draw reasonable conclusions. They had challenged me to be creative not only in writing short stories, but also in taking different points of view about Shakespeare, Blake or Dostoevsky.

There were in my classes at the time some students who wanted primarily to take notes from the board and not engage in discussions about literature. This surprised me, because I thought the most fun with reading was analyzing characters. But some kids who struggled to make the minimum reading requirements felt more comfortable receiving information.

But there were others who enjoyed the give and take of a good argument.

On one occasion, I asked what I thought was a thought-provoking question and was suddenly in shock. Not from the silences that usually greeted me. Those were agonizing and, usually, I just kept on talking!

But on this one occasion in early November, I asked that challenging question, and then one young lady did something that froze me in my tracks as Captain Grant had never done! Leah Panos sat in the center row of all the bolted-down-to-the-floor chairs, the third seat back from my huge oak desk. I asked the question and what did she do?

She stood up in the aisle, feet together and proceeded to deliver a very cogent answer.

I stood there in wonder and apprehension. Would everybody else now stand up to give an answer? Would some of them start walking toward me when they didn't like what I was saying? Would I fumble and flee the stage?

All because slight, dark haired and dark eyed Leah Panos was standing up?

I subsequently learned from one of my colleagues that this was how she and her former classmates in parochial schools responded. They stood up as a sign of respect, not of impending attack. They were taught, as had students in the nineteenth century, to "toe the line," meaning stand straight, toes on a line of the flooring planks, face forward, head high and deliver your recitation.

Good order and discipline is what Leah demonstrated.

Don't always take things at face value is what I learned off Beaufort Island and in that classroom only a year later. Think beneath the surface appearances to the underlying themes, implied messages and hidden verities. We fool ourselves if we rest self-assured with what things seem to be, with surface appearances that mask the subterranean realities.

"The Unknown!"
I'm not sure where my restless discomfort with the way things are usually done came from. Maybe it was my father's continually harping on transforming the hotel reservations systems with his computer. Perhaps it was his repeated denunciations of the word "CAN'T."

"Make your mark in the industry," over and over again until I was sick of it.

"Never, ever give up."

"Bs are never good enough."

"Always travel first class, John. Never settle for anything less." Once when he had to sit back with the common folks, he couldn't stop talking about the pain and suffering he had endured in the after cabin of the DC-3 bouncing over the Rockies.

Maybe I grew into teaching like a maverick who started pushing the teacher's desk to the sidelines because of those words from Captain Scott's journal years ago. It was November, 1903 during his *Discovery* expedition and Scott and his party had traversed the Ferrar Glacier, just west of Hut Point. They trudged forward leaving "the last mountain peak that could remind us of habitable lands." Some men were beginning to fail, to suffer from the constant man-hauling of their wooden sledges beyond this last geological marker and pressed on. What kept them going?

> *. . . before us lay the unknown! What fascination lies in that word. Could anyone wonder that we determined to push on, be the outlook ever so comfortless?*

Or maybe I was emulating both my father and grandfather, one an accountant who dreamed of revolutions in his industry and the other a chemist who worked for years in his laboratory to find the solution to the problems faced by diabetics. His four US patents for D-Zerta, beginning in the year 1925, attest to his amazing success.

Both men set an example of taking the risks involved in pushing back the horizons that circumscribe most of us.

From somewhere during those years of immersing myself in polar literature, I developed a sense of setting off on my own course. Maybe that's why I loved that photo of Little America circa 1929 with somebody's footprints tracing a pathway from foreground to the magic triangle of the radio towers. I wanted to leave my own footprints in the snows.

I hated doing what everybody else was doing, following anything like a prescribed curriculum. There had to be a different course to take toward the goal.

"Don't be a 9 to 5 man," my father always said.

I'm not sure of the origin of this desire to be different, to say and do things somewhat differently from my peers. Maybe everybody feels this way.

At Charles Evans Hughes High School I tried to find ways to get my African-American and Hispanic students involved in good books by asking them "If *you* were Richard Wright what would you have done while working for white men down south in the 1920s?" or "Suppose Macbeth came here to New York and worked for Mayor John Lindsey, what do you think he would have done during the recent garbage strike?" Sometimes the questions sparked lively debate, so lively that the loudness of students' arguments brought not one but several supervisors to my room to check to make sure that things were not totally out of hand, that I was not being threatened with physical violence. They'd walk in and couldn't find me amidst the students shouting --"You're nuts, man, Lindsey ain't no Macbeth!" because I was sitting amongst the students, not standing up front of them lecturing.

"Where's Mr. Barell? Who's driving now?"

Even though arguments between my mother and father upset me terribly back in Needham when I was thirteen and long before that even, I used to love listening to the discussions that my father and grandfather engaged in:

"But Ralph, can't you see that these damned Democratic New Deal policies are driving us to economic ruin? Don't you see that Roosevelt and Truman have given us the beginnings of the welfare state? a socialistic state?"

My father would sit back taking it all in and then say, "O.K., Ray, now can you take the other side of the issue?"

My grandfather, stunned by the question, would rear back, his cigarette ashes arching over mother's carpet like a fishing pole in a deep trout stream, and exclaim, *"Why would I want to do a damned fool thing like that!"*

My father had been on the debate team at Hibbing Junior College, as well as a member of the youth symphony orchestra. And how he loved baiting and attempting to switch my grandfather's reasoning from his Republican point of view to that of the Democrats.

Why would he want to do a damn fool thing like that?

Maybe my father realized that any good thinker needs to be able to consider both sides of the coin, pros and cons of an argument. Set courses often need to be reviewed and modified lest we run aground on false premises.

My students weren't good at taking the other side of the issue either, just lambasting each other with loud canon ball arguments about the virtues of their own ideas--"You're full o' shit, man! Macbeth be just like all them white face dudes down there!"

But we labored toward reasoned arguments over Richard Wright and Shakespeare, only I confess I was thrilled when kids got so heated by their points of view that they could hardly listen to anyone else's ideas.

"There's snow in June!"

After two years of playing with *Black Boy* and *Macbeth*, I moved from the lower west side out to Brooklyn and when I grew weary of experimenting with small groups in a traditional classroom with the chairs screwed down into the oak floors, I started teaching in the alternative school down in the basement of Thomas Jefferson High School on Pennsylvania Avenue in East New York. When I arrived this section of Brooklyn looked like Berlin after World War II, with abandoned buildings on every block, a blight on the borough. Housing here became a focus of President Johnson's "Model Cities" program in the mid 1960s, an effort that was part of his "War on Poverty." Now we were doing battle with the causes of being poor, or were we merely creating different kinds of cement dwellings on the old pastures of Brooklyn? On many an occasion as I set to teaching at 7:20 in the morning, I heard the rooster crowing off in someone's backyard as the sun slowly evaporated the darkness of winter.

The Jefferson Alternative School was housed in the basement of the school and it became a vast experiment with how kids learn. We manipulated everything—-from turning off the hideous bells that rang every 45 minutes to trying to capture the spirit and work of collaboration on film for all to view, analyze and reflect on. We took expeditions to Montauk, set up stores to learn economics, framed out a house right there in the basement and established an internship program for kids in places like IBM, the Brooklyn Museum, Down State Medical Center and the animal hospital on FDR Drive in Manhattan. We wanted students to learn within the community, from experts in their professions engaging in real day-to-day problems, not merely from old textbooks gouged with graffiti.

In New York, June 21st is the summer solstice-- longest day of the year. The sun on this day remains above the horizon longer than on any other day. The days start getting shorter thereafter. In Antarctica June 21st was known as "mid-winter" date, a day of festivities, because winter was half over.

One day early in June our Brooklyn high school students made an astonishing discovery.

We had formed an expedition to the Catskills as part of our outdoor education program. I lugged a video tape camera (and its heavy battery pack and reel-to-reel recorder) all over the mountains to record not only students' discoveries about geology, but we also did it to record their ability to cooperate with each other. My journals for early in the second year record this as one overriding objective, "To learn to live and work together."

Once atop the rocky Catskills hill, we found a large crevasse similar to the ones you might find on the Ross Ice Shelf. My colleague, Stuart Bialer, and several students climbed down inside while I remained up top filming the proceedings.

"Hey, look, man, there's snow down here in June!" shouted one of the kids.

And, indeed, snow had remained since its falling in February or March down in this sheltered igneous outcropping almost up to the longest day of the year in the northern hemisphere.

Upon our return to the basement in Brooklyn, we watched the videos and marked those occasions when we lived up to our ideas of cooperative behavior and those where we needed improvement.

All our efforts were in pursuit of the most authentic learning experiences possible. Without being fully aware of it we were recreating the lives of the intrepid explorers--scientists, dog drivers and naval personnel--all committed to exploring and learning. In order to achieve similar goals, we needed to live and work harmoniously together. My friends and I all believed in the power of cooperation, but I came at this model from the heart of the Antarctic, from Scott, Byrd, Amundsen and Shackleton—from Hut Point, Little America, Framheim and *Endurance*. You couldn't exist for long on the ice if you failed to stay roped together at all times. "NEVER TRAVEL ALONE!"

You had to be ready to lend your warm flesh to a shipmate whose face was becoming speckled with the tell-tale signs of frostbite—those little white blotches here and there.

Little America was the model. Thomas Jefferson Alternate School was the reality.

Chapter Thirteen
Panama Dictator Torrijos

While we were climbing mountains, building businesses and making money, my father was struggling in search of his own south pole in Panama, the Canal Zone, working as a consultant for the Agency for International Development. He was a special assistant to el presidente, Omar Torrijos. He resided at the El Panama Hotel, suite 316 and his office was in the Presidencia, next to the Palace and every morning he had a military car pick him up and take him to work. His stationery was inscribed with the logo of the Office of the President. He was called "The Director General of Planning and Administration, Department of Planning."

How he must have reveled in the heat of the equatorial sun at being "The Director General" of his beloved *Planning*. Planning. "Make your plan and work your plan," he had said over and over and over again *ad nauseam*.

"I love it," he wrote me on his embossed stationery from the Presidencia. He made presentations to general Torrijos' cabinet and, as a result, was hired to implement his vision for expanding tourism in Panama.

But who would want to vacation in Panama City?

On board the heavy cruiser *USS Albany* (CA-123), my Harvard midshipman cruise ship, and onboard *Glacier* I'd already made five journeys through the Canal Zone. I really wondered who would want to set their beach chairs by the Gatun or Miraflores Locks? Who would want to wander down to the gin mills of Balboa or Panama City for a few drinks before relaxing by a hotel pool following the afternoon rains? It always rained in the afternoon here. I couldn't understand his thinking. Just like his beloved RESERVATRON system--"5 seconds from New York to Dallas, John! Can you imagine that!" Yes I could, but why *bother?*

He became involved in negotiations for a canal Zone Treaty. "The Zone is an irritant to the local mentality and has become a mental block of considerable import--!" he wrote in one of his occasional letters.

In Claire Slattery's English class we had read William Blake's poem "London," where he speaks of the "mind-forg'd manacles" he hears in every voice:

> *I wander thro' each charter'd street,*
> *Near where the charter'd Thames does flow,*
> *And mark in every face I meet*
> *Marks of weakness, marks of woe.*
>
> *In every cry of every man,*
> *In every Infant's cry of fear,*
> *In every voice, in every ban,*
> *The mind-forg'd manacles I hear. . .* (Songs of Experience, 1791).

Here were the self-imposed mental blocks of the Panamanians, ripe for my father's brand of CAN-DO entrepreneurship. Never take "NO" for an answer! Don't short suit yourself with notions that you aren't good enough or can't do something. Balls to the wall!

He worked on building a new canal somewhere up north of Panama City to be financed by his "friend" Bob McNamara who had left prosecuting the war in Vietnam and now headed up the World Bank.

Oh, the sweep of his imagination! His dream of access to power at the highest levels fulfilled, at last. He was in his element, like *Glacier* in the pack ice surrounded by playful Adelies, scheming, dreaming on a grand scale.

Recently, my wife and I journeyed to Panama City to visit the El Panama Hotel. There we beheld the huge kidney shaped pool with the covered bar along its edge. How many whiskies had he enjoyed sitting in the shade of Los Palmas, the open air restaurant? As I walked through the lobby and enjoyed the grand open space covered in green/beige Spanish tiles with carved ceramic planters and deep brown leather couches all over, I wondered how many dignitaries he must have met down here. Maybe McNamara, Rusk or the members of Torrijos' cabinet. How often had he dined in Portobello restaurant with its dark mahogany wood trimming?

How often had he gone across the street to the Intercontinental Hotel to drop a few pesos at the card tables? How much money did he actually earn here working for AID?

I never met him here to ask him these questions. My later meetings were conditioned by the status of his health.

With the inevitability of the polar sun's setting upon Little America, this adventure came to a disastrous ending as my father could no longer control his self-destructive passions. I don't know whether Panamanian dictator General Omar Torrijos fired him, but he quickly departed Panama and ended up in a motel in Puerto Rico.

I'll never know General Torrijos was subsequently killed in an airplane crash in 1981, a crash that some have speculated was orchestrated by his successor Manuel Noriega, another General who was captured in 1989 by President George H. W. Bush and who now sits in a Miami jail for drug running.

My father's plans that were finally published in the only book he ever brought to light--*Potential de la Industria de Turismo* with this inscription "A contribution to the years that follow. Dad" Sent to me on my birthday. His final and proud gift to the industry.[23]

Always dreaming of the future, he seemed to live his life deep within visions of tomorrow. Always living well beyond his own horizons. . .he was his own Ulysses. . .but one so severely limited by his own manacles-- Crown Imperial Whiskey with the tiny, *white* seal balancing the little red ball on its nose. . . An Arctic seal. Perhaps a white harp seal. How I loathed that cute little animal back on 23 Webster Park!

A few months after this final and most ignominious departure I picked him up at Newark airport and he was so distorted in girth from his years

---

[23] Just recently I received a beautifully illustrated brochure advertising the wonders of vacationing in Panama. One of Panama's websites (http://www.visitpanama.com/eng/index.php) gives you an idea of the possibilities my father envisioned— "Panama, the path less traveled." Indeed.

of drinking dark whiskey that he looked 15 months pregnant. When I saw him on that Eastern Airlines flight from Puerto Rico, sitting in the front row and unable to rise out of his chair himself, I burst into tears. He failed to recognize me as we drove to New York listening to his favorite concerto, the Mendelssohn. I wasn't sure he even recognized this music.

At Bellevue he kept trying to get to "my meetings with the President," still so full of his illusions of power. His room overlooked the East River and all he did was continue to plan for his meetings with all the CEOs he'd ever met.

On his second day, he looked up at me and said, "You're John?"

He died shortly thereafter and I felt a sad sense of relief for him. I'm not sure now if I cried at his death as deeply as I had upon seeing how his drinking had transformed him into a clownish caricature of the advisor to President Torrijos.

I took his ashes out to the Shinnecock Canal, a few miles from the summer home I shared with my wife Nancy Ann. For some reason I felt that a burial at sea was fitting. As I gently poured out the ashes into the flooding waters of the canal created by the 1938 hurricane (the year he saw me enter the world), I looked up and recalled taking a navigational site on the Shinnecock light marking the canal from the deck of Glacier as we steamed home from our last cruise to Antarctica.

"Mark! 348 degrees true!"

Standing by the canal gently mixing my father's remains with the waters of the Atlantic Ocean, I remembered a colleague of his telling me in the darkest days of his demise that my father was never given credit for his accomplishments, that he felt so painfully the lack of recognition for his beloved reservation system which may just have been a first in his industry.

"They say it can't be done and I tell them they're nuts! Can you believe that, John?"

I didn't care then. I had turned my back on his soaring imagination while in high school. But now I wonder at the palaces he constructed. My anger and despair at his pouring himself so deeply and often down inside any brown pint bottle have subsided and what remains are the mysteries surrounding a life that often seemed a total waste.

How was he able to be so persistent in pursuit of his dream? How in the world did he have enough confidence to tell engineers with PhDs that you could send a signal via computer from New York to Dallas in under five seconds? What in his upbringing had given him the self-assurance that I seemed to lack?

I want to know why I was building ice palaces around Little America while he was dreaming of the CIA and being CEO of any company that would have him. How did our imaginations diverge so drastically? How did we grow up trooping across those strangely unreal and distant landscapes— seemingly so vastly different?

Or were they?

Were we men, young and older, cut from the same quilt?

I don't know. But I would love to ask him. Even now, so many years beyond the dream of Little America and the realities of Vostok and Bellevue.

Now he lingers deep down in my consciousness in ways that surprise me.

How well I recognize that my personal and professional life have been suffused with those messages of assertiveness, persistence, setting goals and high expectations, making a contribution to your industry, your life's work. "Don't be a 9 to 5 man," he always urged. Be different.

"Always give another man a firm handshake. Don't offer him a wet dead fish for a handshake." Always.

But he's also there in my handwriting, when I print out capital letters, he's there in the "B," "R," and "Y." When I hear his beloved Bruch Violin Concerto I understand and feel the passions that surged through his body and frightened me at times and, after a bit too much the sailor's drink, rum, I understand how he began to slip away from us, lose control of his thinking and his speech and drift off into that palace of distorting mirrors where nothing is what it seems to be.

He once counseled me on the meaning of the word "sophistication." I had been using it as a term of high praise in some of my writings.

"You know it really means something else," he said one day.

What?

To be sophisticated also means to be corrupted, to have lost your original purity.

Interesting.

It can mean a debasement of genuineness.

Amazing that I'd been using it in only one way for so long.

He loved words too but never realized that he was living their meanings . . . a loss of the pure spirit he inherited from the iron rich mountains of the Mesabi Range near Hibbing, Minnesota where as a kid he went fishing through the ice of the neighborhood lakes for muskies. It was here during the bitterly cold winters of the north country that he wore that green and black sweater he had given me in Needham. It was here in Hibbing where his first communion was not with his family's Roman Catholic Church but with the artists who fashioned their lives from music, from creating the concertos that he played and those that sent him off into the passions of romance just as they do for me now.

He so often told me that he had become the concert master of the Minneapolis Symphony Orchestra. It was only years later, even beyond my sailings to McMurdo, that I learned he had indeed played the violin but it was for the Youth Orchestra and perhaps in Minneapolis. The photograph we now have, an 8 x 10 black and white with a distinctly yellowish cast of age shows him in 1931 with his violin perched on his knee. On the back it says "Ralph Barell, upon graduation from Hibbing Junior College."

The genuineness of his story lay in his flying far, far beyond the mind-forg'd manacles of Hibbing, 23 Webster Park and his own career in business. Maybe Bruch, Mendelssohn and Beethoven gave him wings to transcend the impurities of his own soul.

Part III: Beyond the Barrier

Chapter Fourteen
"Terrified of flying"

Years after Antarctica's dreams had faded somewhat, mother kept the penguins alive in my mind. On one occasion she sent me the cover from a recent *New Yorker* (September 12, 1977) magazine designed by Charles Addams. Here were Emperor penguins standing around in their rookery with names written across their white breasts: "Wendy, Irv, Ray, Jill, Ted and Helen." Mother had added her own imaginary conversations amongst these strange birds: "Hey, it's John's birthday!. . What class!. .You're looking good!. . .Hey, Man!. . .Have a happy (excuse that expression!)." I did and saved this together with all the other penguin greetings that came every year without fail, even though I cried "Enough! Enough!" I had had enough of Antarctica for the moment when I left McMurdo, but for Betty Barell this was a source of continued fascination and perhaps pride, that her son had traveled such a great distance to fulfill a boyhood dream. Perhaps she had wanted this for me even more than I had! Perhaps this adventure had provided her with an escape from the grimness of her own family life that I never even dreamed of.

But then one day Nancy and I were visiting her in Sherborn (MA) for the weekend. We'd been out to dinner the night before and on this Sunday as we were reading the *NY Times*, she showed me an article that turned my story of Antarctic heroism and camaraderie into the reality I know today.

"Have you seen this review," she asked.

No.

"Oh, it's about Admiral Byrd. I thought you might be interested."

I had not read anything about him or Scott in a while, except an occasional *National Geographic* update on Operation Deep Freeze. I'd been preoccupied with pressing beyond the boundaries of my own teaching as a college professor working with students entering teaching and those searching for new ways to challenge kids to think productively.

I was not expecting what I found in this review of a book by Eugene Rodgers called *Beyond the Barrier* (1990). Here was an account not of the hero I had met and who had urged me to join the greatest adventure of a lifetime, at least not the hero I had created in my own mind. No, here was an account, based on stories his men had written, of a man who was "*so terrified of flying that he was drunk during some of the historic flights on which he was a passenger.*" (emphasis added)

I stopped reading right there. Here it was again! The damned brown bottles of my father's bedroom and all around the house, secreted, hidden, stashed away so nobody but a prowling teenager who desperately wanted to prevent his father's ship from capsizing. . .

WHOOOOOSH! The vicious sea leopard rising from below to gulp the innocent little Adelie penguin right out of his peaceful swim and then thrash him about so severely that his black and white tuxedo of skin would fly off of his little pink and bloody body.

Right in my face. Admiral Byrd had been so drunk in 1929 that he was not even on a flight reported in *Little America* during which Marie Byrd Land was discovered.

Rodgers called him a paranoid liar, suspicious of his subordinates and given to creating a public image of himself vastly different from what his men came to know, someone who suppressed the negative accounts of his behavior as long as he could.

Nixon! Here's another Nixon! I thought. Lies! The pathology of power hidden from the press. We had all lived through the wrenching experience of Watergate in 1973-74, of the discovery of those audio tapes, of the eighteen minute gap, of the "cancer" growing on the White House revealed by John Dean, of the machinations of Haldeman and Erlichman, and, finally, of the discovery of the "smoking gun," the cover-up tape released by order of the Supreme Court and the last gasp, the resignation of a President who said he'd lost his political base of support.

Indeed.

A corruption of the spirit. . .

I was stunned at the report, just as I had been at President Truman's firing of General MacArthur back when I was just discovering Byrd and the South Pole.

I felt as if I'd lost a trusted companion along the pathways of life, someone who had been with me for over forty years now. So far from McMurdo and boyhood images of the magic triangle of radio towers around Little America, I felt a darkness in the pit of my stomach. That terrible feeling of loss, a darkening mass of anxiety deep down. An unwillingness to believe.

Denial.

I denied what I had read, not wanting to damage the image I had nurtured in that closet, en route to 9 Brimmer Street and onboard the decks of *Glacier*. No, I refused to buy the book for months, for over a year.

"Terrified of flying" How could that be? I imaginatively flew along with him, Balchen, McKinley and June on that polar flight. I was *there*. I didn't see or hear anything about fear! Where was it! I doubted Rodgers' account. I was then the embodiment of my mother's skepticism about snow flakes falling down upon LeRoy being unique.

I don't believe it! It can't be true.

Complete denial. No!

"So drunk" When? Where? Must have been after leaving Little America! He couldn't have been anything like my father when I was thirteen, and twenty five and forty. No, he couldn't have been! How I resisted any exploration of these landscapes. I protected the heroic image I had so carefully nurtured during childhood.

Then, several months later, I was working for Zaner-Bloser, a publisher in Columbus, Ohio, on a project for young children called ". . .EVER WONDER. . ?" These little books were designed to help us tap in to children's endless curiosities about their worlds. Perhaps inspired by Einstein's famous thought experiments ("What if I rode along a ray of light. . ?") that I'd written about in my first professional book, *Playgrounds of Our Minds* (1980), I wanted to find ways to challenge young students to ask their own good questions and search for reasonable answers.

Kids wanted to know why penguins walked so funny, why school buses were always yellow and why black holes moved in space. They should have time and opportunity to pose their own questions (within a curricular structure) and pursue answers just as I had done.

I now had more than enough questions about the man I had met so many years before at 9 Brimmer Street. So I journeyed to the Byrd Archives at The Ohio State University Byrd Polar Center in Columbus, OH where all his papers are stored. I wanted at least to pour through some of Byrd's own accounts to find some clues about what actually happened on that adventure.

What amazed me was the sheer volume of records. It seemed as if every radio gram from any ship related to the first two Byrd Antarctic Expeditions was included here, from *The City of New York, Eleanor Bolling, The Bear of Oakland* (Bud Waite's ship), and *The Jacob Ruppert*, Byrd's command vessel in 1933. Here were personal, hand-written letters from Byrd to his wife, Marie, from New Zealand just before the young explorer set sail for the south on his first voyage. So full of longing for her, missing her terribly. The young commander was not all grit and daring, not all plotting courses through the Ross Sea and over the South Pole. His letters to Marie Byrd were those of a young man about to risk his life for science, just as did Wilson, Bowers and Cherry-Garrard back in 1911. But a young naval officer who missed his Marie very, very much.

I had always been intrigued by his sojourn at Advance Base in 1934. Why had he gone alone? I searched through the records trying to find his journal, the source of the book *Alone* (his account of that lonely near death experience) that had kept me reading on and on into the nights when my father was asleep downstairs in front of the smoldering embers of a winter's fire.

I found nothing. But I did find fan letters from all over the world like the one from Myrtle Dean Clark on 12 December, 1938 when I was six months old:

> Alone *is one of my life's treasures--perchance I'll have it buried with me. . .the book is immortal and will go on living. . .I'll show it to St. Peter and he'll say, 'Pretty good, old girl, past sins forgiven. Byrd has given you wings'. . .I feel your great moment is yet to come.*

No wonder I had been so enthralled with this account. It seemed as if people all over the country like Myrtle Clark had loved this book. It had given so many of us our wings to soar beyond our own dead end streets and small plots of land.

But among the hundreds and hundreds of congratulatory letters, there was one that brought back Bud Waite's casual comment while drinking coffee on *Glacier* about who wrote Byrd's books:

> Alone *is glorious, but you know--we both (mom and daughter) wonder if you wrote it yourself or gave your diary and notes to someone else and they wrote it. It does not sound just like you.*

Bud Waite had said that CJ Murphy had written "those books." I heard what he had said so many years ago sitting in the wardroom, but again chose not to listen. Not to believe. And now here was another dissenting voice, another piece of contrary evidence I didn't want to believe. Why had Byrd chosen to keep such a note?

On another occasion while hunting through rare book catalogues I came across an advertised copy of *Little America* inscribed by the Canadian Arctic explorer, V. Steffanson, to the effect that this book of Byrd's had been "ghost written." Who *had* written these books? Similar questions had swirled about the young senator from Massachusetts who had become President. Who *had* written *Profiles in Courage*? President Kennedy, the man who had appointed me to the Naval Academy in 1955 as the result of a state-wide competition? or Theodore Sorenson, his speech writer?

Ghost writers. . .
Appearances. . .

The beguilingly soft surface of the water, but beneath lay the rocks that could ruin your career and the sea leopards that would slice the skin off your back.

The mysteries kept unfolding like spreading ripples from a grain of sand mother had dropped into otherwise placid waters. Like bringing Little Robin into our lives, she was changing my daily reality again.

Finally, I overcame months of denial--months of not wanting to uncover parts of the story that were just too reminiscent of the sun room at 3:30 on school day afternoons. By now my curiosity was peaked and I wanted to know what others knew about what really occurred on the First Byrd Expedition in 1928. I read portions of Rodgers' account, read about the missed flight into Marie Byrd Land because he was too drunk, one he claimed to have been on, flights in preparation for the polar flight where Byrd drank so much brandy that members of the crew had to *sit* on him to keep him under control inside the *Floyd Bennett*, the polar plane. Paul Siple, the twenty year old Eagle Scout, wrote in his diary that night that his commander had "celebrated." Such a different image from that when the plane finally did return from the Pole and the official films show the exuberant explorers carrying the pilots and Byrd off on their shoulders toward their quarters with the polar dog, little Igloo, jumping all about in joyous greeting for his master.

And on July 4th 1929 there was a rousing party with Byrd almost forcing drinks down his fellow explorers and he got so knock-down-drag-out drunk ("three sheets to the wind" as my Navy buddies would say) that he had to be carried back to his bunk saying, "Please don't tell Igloo" about this incident.

The man I idolized, who told me when we met at 9 Brimmer Street in Boston, "You have the smile of a Hollywood actor," this world renowned explorer had the appearance of nobility and daring.

Pure Hollywood.

I was still amazed at being deceived, at believing everything I read. It never occurred to me to ask questions from my closet about the goings on in Little America! Who *would* have?

When I took a course called "Modern Problems" at Wellesley High School with Raymond Chapman, my track coach, we daily read *The New York Times*. Years later I realized that most of my political points of view had been drawn from the editorial pages of this newspaper. I agreed with almost everything Arthur Krock, and later Scotty Reston, had written in their editorial columns. I'd learned what "glittering generalities" were, the meaning of such logical fallacies as *"post hoc ergo propter hoc"* and how to recognize *"bandwagonism," "transfer," "ad hominem"* arguments and other propaganda techniques. But I still believed the editors of *The Times* and had not acquired that healthy skepticism about the conclusions political writers drew about foreign and domestic policies. I was too willing to believe and perhaps this is one reason why my educational career focused in later years on becoming more of a Betty Barell kind of critical thinker, one who possesses a certain skepticism about what to think, believe and do. "Have *you* seen all of the snow flakes that ever fell?"

I wandered through the streets of Manhattan thereafter mourning the loss of my closest companion for many years, the man whose far sightedness had changed my life, encouraged me into the Navy and on down across the Roaring Forties toward the South Pole. I'd lost a part of me.

I still have yet to read the entire account wanting to preserve portions of those landscapes on which he stood so tall in my imagination, leading me and thousands forward toward the unknown.

There was more in the account gleaned from the diaries of his companions, but I never quite got to reading the whole story.

Was the drinking as evident on the second expedition? I recalled hearing something years ago, a rumor I suppose, passed on by one of my shipmates that Byrd's drinking had denied him significant posts during World War II. (What he did do was serve as President Roosevelt's special envoy to the Pacific in search of suitable landing sites.) That little report had been only partially buried, together with others Bud Waite had mentioned that smudged the heroic figure's glow in my mind.

But time is a funny apparition, a figment of our imaginations that plays with our minds in strange fashions. The more I reflected on my own explorations, recalling my flights of discovery and camaraderie with my former shipmates on *Glacier*, the more I became fascinated with these diaries Rodgers had used. Where were they? How could I confirm his findings for myself?

Chapter Fifteen
Remembering
22 November, 1963

So one warming spring day in late March just before an educational conference I crossed Pennsylvania Avenue in Washington, D.C. en route to the National Archives there to read the diaries of members of the second Byrd Antarctic Expedition, those of Bud Waite, Thomas Poulter, and Pete Demas, his rescuers during that fateful winter of 1934.

I strode across Pennsylvania Avenue that morning brimming with excitement, the passion of the historian about to uncover stories untold for decades. Search for the data and dispel the stories and myths, Apsley Cherry-Garrard had said as he ventured off from Cape Evans in search of the Emperor penguin eggs.

The history of this Avenue was hard to ignore as I waited for the light. I had been driving in 'Loft Conn through the seemingly endless and boring McMurdo bay ice, when Don Epperson, who had relieved me as Communications Officer when I was promoted to Operations Officer, climbed up and handed me a message from a weather bureau teletype. "Commander-in-Chief shot in Dallas." Godalmighty, I thought. Who's that? Commander-in-Chief of Pacific operations? SecNav? No, it was the President! I couldn't believe it! The shock of that message was more intense than the most glaring sun rays reflected off the bright white surfaces all around me. We had our

Presidents and, except for Lincoln, they served their country and lived. Shot in Dallas. And then word came that President John F. Kennedy had died.

Shot from behind, in the head, we lost the man who would have sent me to the Naval Academy, the man who seemed to embody all our dreams about service and sailing through dangerous waters. Taking the risks and standing up to the Soviet Union in the Cuban Missile Crisis. A man of bold stripe and daring, bloodied like one of those little Adelie penguins caught unawares from behind by a jawing leopard seal and thrashed to death.

President Kennedy's caisson came down this road drawn by the single stallion as a stunned nation watched on television--the slain leader who personified so much of a nation's hopes for youthful regeneration through his establishing a Peace Corps.

I remembered the disbelief of that November day in McMurdo high above the ice hearing that the Commander-in-Chief had been slain. The Presidency had always seemed to be an inviolate office. Presidents lived out their terms. Some institutions seemed impervious to change--the Yankees, Notre Dame football team, MacArthur. . . But no longer. (I had momentarily forgotten about Lincoln, Garfield, and McKinley)

"Now hear this!" came Captain Vaughan's voice over the ship's 1 MC "This is the Captain speaking. We have just received word from the Secretary of the Navy that our Commander-in-Chief, President Kennedy, was slain in Dallas. We have no further details. That is all."

Curt, abrupt. . . just like a gun shot in Dallas.

Whenever I thought about Kennedy during the remainder of my service on *Glacier*, I was in tears or close to it. I couldn't accept the fact that someone so handsome, so young, so vibrant had been taken from us. More and more he seemed like the meteor that flashes through your atmosphere—-bright, shining and unalloyed. But he flamed out at the hand of a man who may have been a Communist. Not even a civil rights worker—a Communist.

Golden Wedding Whiskey in Little America
And then I sat in the National Archives in a room with very high ceilings and windows through which the sun shone so brilliantly upon the grey government cartons of papers, diaries and newspaper clippings from the past. Here were more stories to read to discern fact from public image. And here was an amazing

document written by Dr. Thomas C. Poulter, chief scientist and second in command of the Second Byrd Antarctic Expedition. Entitled "The Winter Night Trip to Advance Base, Byrd Antarctic Expedition II 1933-35" Poulter in 1973 told the story of his battle with another polar pilot, Harold June, who had wanted to be second in command, but who Byrd felt drank too much. Indeed, June had brought to Little America a very large secret stash of liquor. Poulter confiscated some of it and buried it in one of Little America's tunnels, those childhood fortresses of safety and security from the storms that swirled throughout 23 Webster Park.

Defiling the spirit of magic I had created from that closet so long ago, June wanted his liquor every evening, just like someone at home.

When Poulter got word that June was out "to get TCP" if he had to "wreck the expedition" to do it, he decided he had to act quickly.

Mae Millikin's history class had been exciting, but nothing like actually doing history with the Spring sunlight streaming in through the huge windows overlooking Pennsylvania Avenue. I had never read such gripping material.

Poulter moved all of the liquor into his meteorological shack:

> *I drilled a hole through the floor and put a large glass funnel in it and started dumping Golden Wedding Whiskey. When I went into the tunnel the odor of whiskey was very strong so I changed my procedure. After a few fifths I would dump some chlorinated lime in the hole and burn some wool in the tunnel to mask the odor. I eventually dumped 500 fifths of Golden Wedding down that hole. I thought I knew how a murderer felt when he hadn't figured out ahead of time what he was going to do with the body, for the bottles occupied just as much space empty as full.* (TCP, 1973)

Raskolnikov! Another hero. Right here on the ice.

The tunnels I wandered around in with so much admiration for their precise and perpendicular lines through which I imaginatively prowled ever alert for the comradely conversations about plans for the next spring's sledging operations to the Queen Maud Mountains or into Marie Byrd Land, these same tunnels had been the scene of the most massive alcoholic deception in polar history. Harold June's determination to find his beloved whiskey led him to poke through those perpendicular snow walls with six foot rods trying to find this cache of Golden Wedding Whiskey, a cache with enough bottles in it for each man to have *ten* bottles during the winter months of isolation. June and my father! What a companionship of the bottle!

And the Christmas card pictures of Little America with those footprints leading from foreground toward the three radio towers, all these pictures of men so warmly discussing plans and future operations, now became suspect as I left the National Archives. I wondered how many of those photographs that I had studied so carefully up in my little closet over the sun room had been staged for Joe Rucker and Willard Van der Veer of Paramount Pictures. In how many of them did the men have severe hangovers from serious bouts of revelry the evening before? How many men nearly died from being dead drunk in the tunnels? What could you believe about the published reports of these and other expeditions? The film made from all of the Paramount photos taken during the first expedition was haled by *Variety* Magazine as "Only bona fide drama and authenticity prevail. . .The photography is a work of art."

Several years ago my sister Missy gave me a framed poster advertising the Paramount movies of Little America touting the "Daring" of these men:

> *The greatest story of adventure ever filmed! A true record of terrifying exploits and unflagging courage in uncharted lands of the greatest danger. Paramount's exclusive sound and talking wonder picture, two years in the making, including actual scenes of Rear Admiral Byrd flying over the South Pole! Sheer, stark drama that will hold you breathless from the start, give you something to talk about for weeks and remember all your life! The greatest expedition of modern times—and it is only natural that its filming was entrusted to the greatest organization in motion pictures.* (from *The Saturday Evening Post* of June 14, 1930*)*

But how severely had art distorted authenticity?

Hollywood. . .Appearances. . .Stories imagined. . .Dreams dashed upon sub-surface rocks and down partially hidden crevasses. . .Byrd wasn't what he seemed to be. . .

But neither was Antarctica. Now we also have reason to believe that Antarctica had once ranged far to the north. She was, it turns out, once "married" to portions of the North American continent. Geologists Ian Dalziel (University of Texas) and Eldridge Moores (University of California) believe that portions of the East Antarctica coast line contain a "band of 1.1 billion year old metamorphic rocks very similar to the so-called Grenville belt that runs from Texas through the Adirondack Mountains of New York."[24]

So, Antarctica had once upon a time snuggled up against the dusty plains of Texas and the slopes of the ancient Blue Ridge Mountains of Virginia, wherever they had lain over 600 million years ago.

The mysteries abound.

There would have to be a reckoning. And there was.

---

24 Richard Monastersky, 1991 "Married to Antarctica," *Science News*, Vol. 139. April, 27. P. 266

Chapter Sixteen
At last a reckoning

On the Amtrak train from Washington to New York the next day I continued to savor the feelings of excitement, awe and wonder in front of the diaries of men I had read about so many years before. Reading history with Canoni and at Harvard had never, *ever* been as thrilling, had never brought me so close to the men who made the most important story in my life, men who had risked everything, fought, drank and nearly died were here spinning their own yarns. Stories to devour as if they were a full meal for a man near starvation. Stories that spoke so loudly beyond the words on the pages, because they gave a totally different picture from what I understood.

Here they came alive on the thick oak tables of the National Archives in the brilliant spring sunshine streaming through the high windows, their hand written and typewritten memoirs for all to read and disclose more of what actually occurred in the winter of 1934. It was like being with them in a way even more intense than I had felt as a thirteen year old wondering what they were like, were they good students, how did they become members of the expedition. It had never occurred to me then, or even a year previous, to wonder how much liquor they had secreted away with them on the *Bear of Oakland* as she pushed through the pack ice en route from New Zealand to the Bay of Whales. It had never occurred to me that some of them would behave just like the father dead drunk on the day bed back at 23 Webster Park, or as we so often said on *Glacier*, shit-faced. . . and fucked up beyond all recognition." It never occurred to me to consider the possibility, to ask the question.

So many stories, so many seeming distortions that struck me as if with a blow to my stomach. That's where I felt the loss--no, not the loss but the change in a companion who had ridden with me on the journeys from Needham, Wellesley, Cambridge and Christ Church, New Zealand. I thought I had lost someone who had invited me to explore, to participate in humankind's greatest adventure, opening new territories never before seen or trod upon.

But eventually I realized that on those occasions when the Captain and the Executive Officer had flown off Glacier for a party at McMurdo Station, on New Year's Eve and on other occasions, my shipmates and I stole down below to one officer's cabin near the water line, cracked open a few bottles and had us a merry old time. My super 8mm movies of those *Glacier* days vividly show us down in lower officer's quarters drinking with an Argentinean officer who was an observer on board. Very clearly you can see the bottle of Tia Maria and there must have been others sitting down on deck. The date was New Year's eve, 1963. "Keep your doppers up," Captain Grant had said. And raise your glasses high!

Had we been observed, we could have been subject to military court martial and dismissed from the service immediately. My shipmates and I loved to drink and we were willing to break Naval Regulations on certain occasions to do so. When I resigned from active duty in the Navy I loved rum and coke, then scotch and bourbon and then back to rum, the sailor's drink. It still worries me that I have the potential for my father's kind of boozing. There must be something in the genes, I think.

So we aren't so different after all. Were I cooped up for months of darkness with lots of other men, I would certainly have my promenades on the ice shelf, but also a case or two or three of Mt Gay Rum from Barbados and some way to frolic with my very own *Esquire* women of yesteryear.

And like the men of the imaginary expedition I created years ago in "Twenty Below," I might have become so enraged at one of my companions that, like Norman Vaughan (the Harvard drop-out who served in 1928 as a young dog driver), I would have escaped topside during the winter night in a tent to avoid being murdered by Joe Walden, the chief dog driver. The older driver was angry enough, perhaps out of jealousy, that he seemed intent upon becoming another Raskolnikov, bludgeoning his victim with a pistol not the ax that the young Russian student used against the old pawn broker in Dostoevsky's *Crime and Punishment*!

Murder in the magic triangle certainly would have "wrecked the expedition"!

Several years ago I purchased one of the two scrapbooks kept since 1928 by Byrd's secretary. On the cover is a sepia drawing of him just like the one in Little America, the high cheek boned profile looking up and off into the distance, imagining another horizon to conquer. I still see him every day as a leader, companion and friend with both feet deeply embedded in the snows of human struggle and weakness.

Imagine the courage it took just to climb aboard an airplane if you're terrified of flying! Everybody troops through the same snows at one time or another. . .

But how could I have believed everything I had read? How could I have fashioned this man and his community Little America into some kind of polar paradise?

The answer is that I *had* to. . .

I needed Antarctica and Little America and Byrd and all his men so much more than I needed anything taught in Needham Junior High School. And later I needed Gethsemani. . .the gardens of Thomas Merton where he saw Heaven in every wild flower and belonged to a community of men of reverent stripe who surrounded him with love and purpose. After Byrd Merton had become another hero as a Trappist monk who escaped from the sins of Greenwich Village and the horrors of World War II.[25]

Yes, stories comfort and succor us in times of turmoil, providing us with sanctuaries from the storms that rage around us.

But stories do so much more than provide us with escape tunnels. The pioneer explorers and the men and women who marched down Pennsylvania

---

25 At some point I read Merton's *Seven Storey Mountain*, an account of his conversion to Roman Catholicism and his venturing into the Trappist Monastery at Gethsemani, Kentucky. And like all of the polar explorers, I avidly read most everything this young contemplative and scholar of monasticism wrote in his short life. Sometimes I wonder about what conjoined both Byrd and Merton in my mind--perhaps exploring new dimensions of life, being alone, and having deep commitment to personal goals.

Avenue and those who threw rocks and bottles at tanks in Budapest during the 1956 uprising against Communism were continually telling us that we could become our own authors, tell our own stories and live out our own dreams. Their stories told us that we do not need to suffer under the oppression of those who work their autocratic powers against the will of the people. The telling of our own story is our liberation from the childhood games of Canoni, a liberation from the shackling fear of doors that most surely would have opened had we the courage to knock.

Telling our own stories is our way of climbing up to the conning towers of our own ships, taking the engine controls firmly in hand and saying, "Balls to the Wall!"

Stories soften us into the selves we become down through the seasons of life. . .

Yes, stories inspire. . .and that leads me back to my mother. . .

Chapter Seventeen
The Infinite Sandbox

From an airport in Raleigh, North Carolina I called Mother recently to tell her how much I appreciated her love and steadfastness during all the years of my growing up. I had just finished a workshop and a teacher had remarked on its quality. I asked what made it so good. You, the participant said. I wanted my mother to hear those words since she was just as responsible for creating the foundation for who I am as was my father.

During the same conversation she told me for the first time that she was not sorry to see me leave for Harvard so many years previous. We had earlier spoken of how Little Robin, now the mother of three of her own children, was saddened by the forthcoming departure of her oldest son, Alden, for college. Well, I wasn't sorry to see you get out of there, Mother said, referring to the rage of emotional storms that governed our lives then. She was glad that someone was escaping the turbulence that caused the ship of our family to founder so continuously. She was not sorry, but that meant that she had one fewer allies at home.

It wasn't until I was in my last year of high school that we together confronted the reality of my father's drinking. "Perhaps we should have spoken of this earlier," she said sadly. Yes.

I recalled so many other conversations with her from airports around the country, ones where I had called to tell her that I had told her part in this story to educators. After receiving the degree my father always coveted, the doctorate, from Teachers College, I had begun to work with young people who wanted to become teachers, attempting to show them how to challenge students to use their heads for more than hard disk memory storage devices, to use them to think through real problems that mattered.

My mother's story takes me back to those days of being thirteen and her mother, Florence Wright Ferguson, suggesting I might want to read Byrd's story for a book report. Part of my mother's story is how that book and each succeeding one sparked my curiosity to the extent that I wanted to find out all about these explorers, why they sailed south, what they found and, just as importantly, what they'd done with their lives since 1930 or 1935.

Her story involves urging me to write Byrd himself. I probably demurred giving excuses like "He's probably too busy" to cover my own diffidence. But with her support and that of my English teacher, Mrs. O'Leary, I sat down and penned the letter, the rough draft of which I still have today.

And I waited so impatiently for a reply. I came home from school every day hoping there would be a response, but for so many depressing weeks, as winter's snows melted into the food for spring's early daffodils, there was nothing. No word from the Admiral living at 9 Brimmer Street in Boston.

What I didn't know was that she had sat down and written Admiral Byrd herself expressing to him her son's deep interest in his work. And completely hidden from me during so much of my growing into the person who held Byrd in such high esteem was the fact that the first letter from 9 Brimmer Street, Boston came not to "Master John Barell," but to "Mrs. Ralph James Barell." Here is what Byrd said:

Dear Mrs. Barell

Of course I will write your son and it will be a real pleasure to do so. Naturally it pleases me very much to have youngsters interested in me and my doings.

You are right in telling your son that I have been away. In the first place, until now I haven't been back to my home in Boston since Christmas.

I have an office in Washington and when I am doing any desk work I am at that office most of the time.

Don't tell John about this letter, for I will write him as soon as I can find his letter.

With best wishes,

Sincerely,

(signed) *Richard E. Byrd*

Mother adhered to his wishes for many, many years, not wanting, she told me while I waited for a plane home, to think that she had interfered with my project, my ardent dream. She had wanted me to have a man like Byrd to admire. Perhaps she felt her son's anxiety as he came home to an empty mail box and, upon occasion, to the sight of his father sprawled out on the day bed with the sun streaming through the beige curtains she so neatly arrayed across the walnut casements. Her own life's companion was slipping away from her so surely and so sadly. Perhaps she wrote the letter in between the migraines she suffered that laid her out for an entire day or more. On so many occasions I stood by her bedside in the darkened bedroom completely helpless, wanting very much for her to be up making breakfast, not because I was hungry but because that's what she did in the morning. That's what she was supposed to be doing. That was the routine Missy, Robin and I depended upon.

And so, had mother not written that letter this whole unfolding story would never have taken place. Byrd did find my first of so many letters and wrote me the following day. Amazing. The mysteries keep unfolding.

And there had been another surprise! During the final days of the second Reagan administration on one of my expeditions to the Archives of the Byrd Polar Center at Ohio State University I made another discovery. I methodically searched through the index of all Byrd's records and there in Folder 1103, Box 26 I found the following: "Barell, John. Correspondence. 1953." He had kept all the letters I sent and the carbons of those he mailed out. He also the 3 x 5 photograph I sent him that mother had taken, the one that almost did not materialize because of the finicky batteries. There it was—the "Hollywood smile" preserved in better condition than my own, tattered, almost torn-in-half copy kept these fifty years in my own archives.

Now I understand that those who dwell within the quieter spaces of our lives lead and sustain us in ways that our so-called heroes do not. I realize that when we become mesmerized by the flash and daring of our so-called heroes, we overlook the quiet love of those who write the letters, make the thousands upon thousands of peanut butter and jelly sandwiches and tuck us into our dreams every night as predictably and reassuringly as the next day's dawn. And we might never understand the courage it took to leave home in search of work after so many years in the kitchen, to knock on the doors and ask for a job, to accept the refusals and to press on to eventual success. To overcome those dreadful, body-numbing migraines that kept you under the covers and arise the next day to quietly sell your professional skills to total strangers while your kids are in school and your partner might still be home, on the day bed, snoring, dead drunk, so tragically off course that few navigators could even orient him toward his rightful bearings, toward his own north or south pole.

It is only now, after spending so many hours remembering and writing that I begin to feel mother's daily struggle to keep scrambled eggs, meat loaf and my favorite dessert, tapioca, on the table whenever we wanted them. Our own pains we can soon forget or grow beyond. Memory doesn't hang onto the sensation of suffering. But feeling someone else's grief is never easy and Betty Barell seemed to keep hers from us, except for those migraine headaches. Yes, there were loud arguments that always scared me—"If you ever go to work like that again, Kelsey will fire you!"-- and I was always there worrying and listening, down the corridors in Hartsdale, through the walls in Needham and Wellesley. Will he leave us? Will he be fired? How will we survive?

But had mother not been there to steady the rudder of our family's ship during her own personal agonies and despairs, we all surely would have been washed out to sea without those life rings of decency, wonder and devotion.

Now I realize that without her surrounding me with love, I would never have had that playground upon which to fashion the palaces of possibility so many years ago. She stood by the infinite sandbox encouraging me to immerse myself in the exploits of those men of bold stripe and daring, urging me to troop across the landscapes they had delineated and to plunge on beyond the

Chapter Seventeen: The Infinite Sandbox

horizon into the realm of the unknown. She proof-read all the letters that I sent to Byrd, to Balchen, to survivors of Scott's Last Expedition and to the Federal Government in search of the rights to a few acres of land at the base of Mt. Grace McKinley. She was the one who asked if I wanted to send out a letter to the "US Navel Department."

Yes, she was the one who helped bring these dreams to fruition and she was the one who made their reality unbelievably and painfully accurate in the end.

And just when I thought there were no more memories locked away in closets of her home, there came in the mail a picture.

There she was. . .

The City of New York. . .The picture I had mounted on cardboard under glass with red tape around the edges and placed next to the chart of Antarctica signed by Admiral Byrd. Mother found it amongst all her papers. Like the image of the burned out ship, the picture had become crinkled and cracked in the half century since the Yarmouth photographer sent it to me. There was *The City,* no longer Herculean, but her sides were still of 34 inch oak and spruce, "of the finest cut."

Ships make waves and leave a churned up white water wake often full of brilliant blue-green phosphorescence. This ship had steered me south so often and the wake I left in my own life had been guided by my mother. She had become the first and final pilot.

And then there was Paul Siple, the Eagle Scout, the youngest member of the First Byrd Expedition, the young man I admired so because of his youth, daring and presence on this expedition.

In a telephone call to my aunt, Anne living outside of Tucson, I happened to mention a recent blizzard and the name of Paul A. Siple, the Boy Scout with Byrd in 1928.

My mother was standing close by and upon hearing Siple's name, she said rather nonchalantly, "Oh, I met him."

Again! The discoveries!

"When?" I asked in amazement.

"When I was sixteen. He came to my high school."

"In LeRoy?"

"Yes."

So for over fifty years I had thought that I was the first person in my family to connect with one of the members of Byrd's First Antarctic Expedition. No.

> *I imagined my mother, aged sixteen, sitting in an auditorium in Le Roy High School (New York, between Rochester and Buffalo), when the principal announced, "Our guest speaker for this morning is a young man we could all aspire to be like, the youngest member of the Byrd Antarctic Expedition, Eagle Scout, Mr. Paul Siple."*
>
> *Elizabeth Lockwood Ferguson sat there with all her girlfriends dressed in her sweater, skirt and saddle shoes listening as the tall, slender, young Scout (now about 21 years old) enthralled his audience with a story about being selected to sail with Byrd, about his thrill in working with the sailors on* The City of New York, *teaching them all the sea-going knots he already knew, about being one of the several dog sled leaders, along with Norman Vaughan, a young Harvard drop-out. He told about killing seals and penguins for fresh meat and about Byrd's historic flight over the South Pole and what that meant for the history of polar exploration.*
>
> *He would have brought his fur parka, mukluks for tramping through the snows on the Ross Ice Barrier and a few photographs with him and the Adelie and Emperor penguins.*
>
> *"What was your happiest moment?" one student asked.*
>
> *"Seeing the sun come back to Little America," he said with a broad smile." The seasons down there are reversed and we spent four months in total darkness."*

"And he signed my notebook," my mother added.

"Where is it?" I asked knowing full well the answer.

"Oh, I don't know," she said laughing about the intervening seventy two years of not keeping track of the yellow notebook with Siple's signature.

Almost three quarters of a century ago, seven years before I was born, my mother had the interest to seek out Siple, to get his autograph, seeing in this young adventurer someone to admire, someone who sailed the seas in search of the unknown. She got up out of her auditorium seat, approached the stage and, I'm sure so politely, asked, "Mr. Siple, may I have your autograph?"

Sure, he would have said, signing his name in the upper right hand corner near the names of some of her friends in the class of '31.

My mother, the first adventurer in the family.

Without her there would be no story. . .

A spirit, pure, shining, adventurous and unsophisticated. . .

And these stories of our growing up, fashioned within the playgrounds of our minds, disclose the mysteries that swirl in and around our lives and soften us into the adults we are--so much more than we seem to be. . .but less than we could be.

19. Elizabeth, Marcia, Ray, Anne and Wright Ferguson.

20. *Elizabeth Lockwood Ferguson Barell with her first born.*

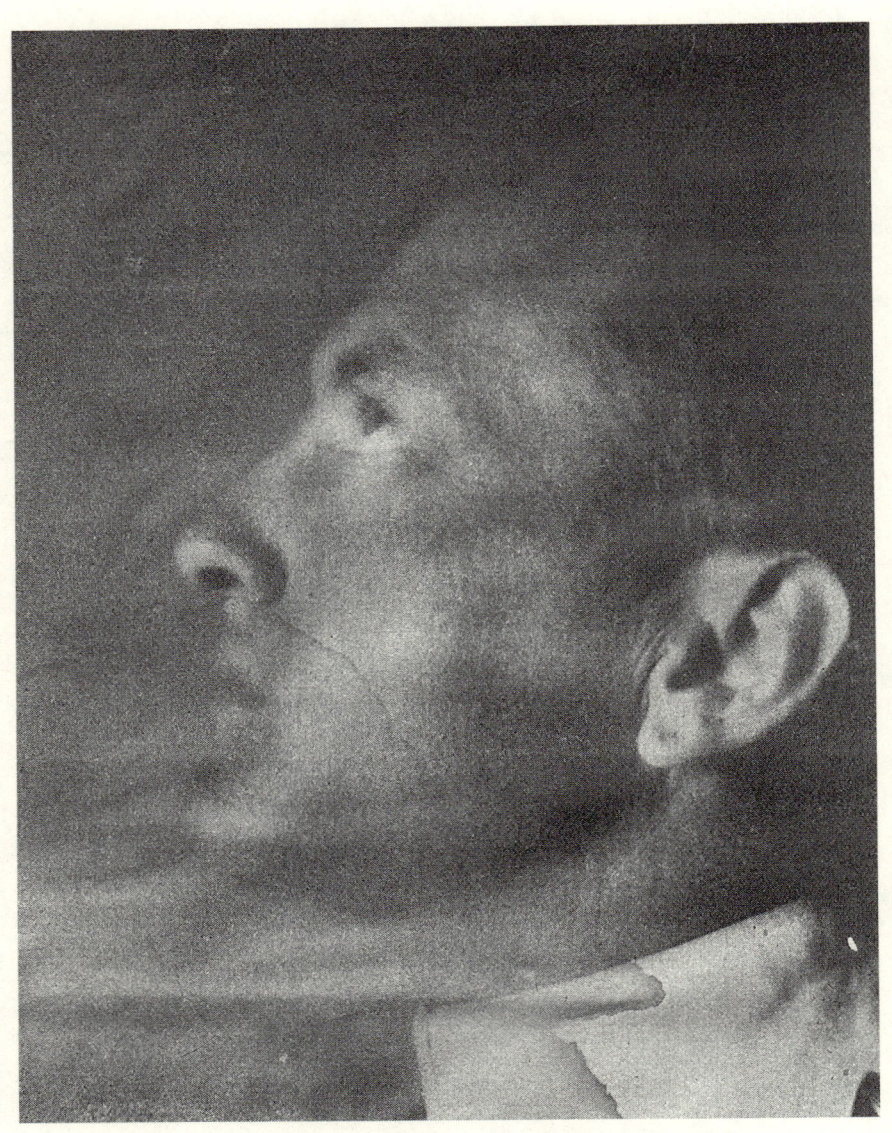

21. *Admiral Byrd on cover of scrapbook kept by one of his secretaries.*

Afterword
A View from the Conning Tower

On a warm California day in June of 2000, I slowly climbed the steps inside the darkened mast of my former home, a ship that had fulfilled my boyhood dreams of sailing south to magical landscapes full of mystery, camaraderie and daring.

I took each step very cautiously—one step for each year since serving on board what we called "the free world's most powerful icebreaker." There were 35 rungs on the ladder, one for each year of my professional life after the Navy, teaching young people how to probe the universe for answers to their own questions.

The shaft felt narrow and cramped and I wondered how much I had changed since my years of service. Now I was climbing up to the conning tower, the enclosed, black box on the mast of *USS Glacier* from which we drove the ship while exploring the ferociously windblown and elusive coastlines of Antarctica. Reclaimed by the Glacier Society from the Navy, *Glacier* sat in the Sacramento River surrounded by hundreds of other ships in the reserve fleet. Not too far away was the USS *Iowa*, a battleship that had served in World War II, and Korea.[26]

---

[26] Glacier Society, (www.glaciersociety.org) under the leadership of Ben Koether, worked for several years to raise money for *Glacier*'s refitting and eventual service in the Arctic in pursuit of humanitarian goals. As of this writing the mission appears not to have been successful, unfortunately for the thousands of volunteers who worked tirelessly to bring our ship back to readiness.

The opening into what we called 'Loft Conn was a lot smaller than I remembered it and I wondered how my shipmates, men of larger stature than I like Dryden and Rice, managed to squeeze through. When I once again stood in the master command post positioned on the mast one hundred feet above the water line, I recalled spending relentless hours driving through almost limitless seas of intensely white pack ice with those elegant ladies of the sea, tabular icebergs, bathed in pinks and lavenders, captured in an iceman's iron grip.

Now on this sunny California day my first impressions gazing out the windows were of the colorful scenery, the golden hills surrounding Benicia, the rusting ships to port and starboard, the brilliant blue June sky and the white superstructure of the ship. She'd been haze gray in 1963 and now in 2001 she was a dirty Coast Guard red. (All Navy icebreakers had been transferred to the Coast Guard in 1966)

The Sacramento River is a dark muddy brown from up here and the speculation by men conducting ship's restoration on *Glacier* was that she was probably sitting on the river bottom. This was not surprising since others had said that the river annually transfers six feet of silt downstream, building up sediments that ever so slowly reshape California's coastlines.

On our port side was a very old, paint peeling off her superstructure oil barge, listing slightly to port looking worse than the *African Queen*.

To starboard was an ammunition ship retired as recently as five years ago, having served during the height of the cold war, when the Soviet Union was the "Evil Empire." The ammunition ship had then carried atomic bombs across the Pacific and into ports where they were, by international agreement, forbidden. Her spaces were still clean, her brite work (the brass fittings) still shining in her darkened spaces below and on her bridge.

Just before re-boarding *Glacier* for the first time on this day in June since 1964, I had asked Jack Erhard, engineer in charge of restoration, about the ships alongside.

"One's a beat up old cargo carrier and the other's an ammo ship."

Ammunition? Ships that deliver huge bombs to the fleet.

"Which one is she?" I asked trying to remember the various names I'd learned years ago—Mona Loa, Haleakala, Vesuvius?

"*Mauna Kea*," said Jack nonchalantly.

"*Really?*" I said in disbelief.

"Yea, why?"

"That was the first ship I was assigned to out of college back in 1960."

The coincidence was almost too amazing for words. Here was Captain Hart Dale Hilton's ship, *USS Mauna Kea* (AE-22), the ship that "touched" bottom on this very same Sacramento River so many years ago now lying alongside *Glacier*. She too had been decommissioned, her name and number removed from the ship's hull. Only a decal painted on the side of one of her main deck bulwarks displayed her proud name, derived as with most ammunition ships, from the name of a volcano.

Many of the watches I'd stood up here in 'Loft Conn were spent driving through the Ross Sea pack ice toward McMurdo Sound watching the Weddell seals roll over lazily as we barged by, and seeing penguins, both Adelie and Emperor, rocket out of the polar seas from depths of 800 feet to land on their webbed feet or their ample, blubber enriched bellies. Back then few, if any, worried about the survival of these precious animals always decked out in their black and white finery. Now we know our blue planet's once stable systems are changing, some deteriorating--her oceans are warming and huge Connecticut-sized icebergs are calving off the Ross Ice Shelf adversely affecting the food supplies of these elegantly attired hosts of all explorers' who visit their natural habitats. Those tiny air bubbles below Vostok tell the story of earth's changing atmospheric conditions and human's contribution thereto.

But most of my time here I stood on these narrow deck plates and peered out the rectangular windows, each with its own heater and window wiper, gazing south toward our ultimate destination, Hut Point, cutting through ten feet of bay ice on a course of 147 degrees true. This jet black volcanic peninsula jutting into McMurdo Sound is where Captain Robert Falcon Scott, in his first expedition to Antarctica, purposefully froze his ship *Discovery* into the winter bay ice to serve as shelter in 1901. On our port side was a smoking Mt. Erebus, what we thought was the only active volcano in Antarctica.

Why, I wondered then, was there only one volcano on the continent? Now we know there are others hidden beneath thousands of feet of glacial ice making these polar plateaus even more unstable. Scientists worry that the West Antarctic Ice Sheet (between the Bay of Whales and Palmer Peninsula) will collapse into the sea raising water levels to such heights that one third of Florida would become submerged. This ice sheet had already disappeared once in the past 600,000 years and may do so in the not too distant future.

Surface stabilities are very misleading when it comes to polar ice shelves and glaciers.

On this sunny deep blue-sky morning I took hold of the round throttles on a square box that drove the ship's twin screws with 21,000 horsepower through the ice. I could almost hear Captain Ed Grant barking at me through the 21 MC communications system from down on the bridge, "C'mon, Barell, goose her!" And I learned how to do that under his leadership, to take control of the ship, not to shrink from using all that power to plow a course through the ice to bring scientists closer to discovering answers to their questions about earth's mantle and the tectonic forces moving continental plates across the globe.

With the throttles in my hands now I could still feel the excitement of command, sharing with the Captain in the leadership of this expedition. Driving through the heavy bay ice of McMurdo, relentlessly attacking it to create a passageway for re-supply ships, gave me a thrill even more intense than those days when I first drove our black Ford around Wellesley, Massachusetts so many years ago finally free from parental supervision on the highways.

I counted the windows—seven in all—because I had spent so much time watching the sea and bay ice in its endless fascination, here flat as a desert mesa, there hummocked up with pressure sufficient to have crushed Shackleton's immense dream of marching across the continent from the Weddell Sea to McMurdo.

I walked from one side to the other, a distance of four paces, counting them to remember how I spent four hours up here relentlessly pounding the ship's gross tonnage of 9,000 tons up onto the ice so she would crush it. How many times I'd stood on the ice and watched that spectacle, feeling the vibrations through my feet the way elephants standing on African savannas sense danger through the soles or toenails of their feet.

I was alone in 'Loft Conn for this moment. My wife Nancy was below working to clean up the bridge. It was filthy and had had dead birds scattered here and there when volunteers of the Glacier Society first boarded her two years previous. We were on board on a June day at the turn of the century to restore her to sailing trim and outfit her for humanitarian services to indigenous peoples in the Arctic.

As part of the ship's restoration the volunteers spent many, many hours scavenging equipment from other ships in the Reserve Fleet. We liberated tons of equipment: battle lanterns, spare motors, miles of cable, VHF and UHF antennae, silverware for the wardroom and mess decks and on one trip back to *Mauna Kea*, I found a perfectly serviceable compass repeater up on the bridge where Captain Hilton had ordered "All Back Emergency!" We had already removed the gyro compasses from *Mauna Kea*.

On one of the largest scavenging expeditions we cut loose an emergency generator from my former home, tore open a hole in her hull and hoisted it aboard *Glacier*. We were refurbishing our own ship acquiring as much pre-paid equipment as possible.

Glacier had been decommissioned in 1987 and sent up river there to be watched over monthly by a crew from the Maritime Administration until the Navy saw fit to bury her deep down in the Pacific. When in the early 1990s I had inquired about my former ship at the Bureau of Ships in Washington, a seaman told me she was to become "a large target," meaning she'd be towed out to the Pacific and used as target practice for young gunners' mates. But then Glacier Society intervened.

She was now dark in her interior spaces now. No one had lived aboard for all those years. No one had risen at the crack of dawn to swab her decks, to cook breakfast for a hungry crew of officers, men and scientists. Down on the bridge where Nancy was cleaning the windows she passed by the *Glacier*'s magnetic compass, also scavenged from *Mauna Kea*. The ship's course on this compass registered 000 degrees north—magnetic. But as Koether noted previous volunteers had installed her backwards (with the flinders bar pointing aft).

We were in Row E of retired vessels and in Row G was the battleship *Iowa*, BB-61 with her sixteen inch guns that had fired projectiles over twenty miles in land during the Persian Gulf War. *Iowa* was almost ready to sail. There were other retired naval vessels with their names painted over, and some merchant ships that had sailed during previous campaigns where supplies were vitally needed.

There were cargo vessels with names like *Dawn*, *Adventure* and *Ambassador*.

I looked out the forward most window in this black conning tower sitting just below ebony tear drop platforms that had carried our surface search and air search radars, ANSPS 10 and 6C, if I remember their designations correctly. I gazed down the Sacramento River and back in to history, back thirty five years to my first setting eyes on *Glacier* in a Wellington, New Zealand dry dock where her broken screws were being replaced. There I beheld her watermelon-shaped hull designed to resist the pressures of the pack ice that could immobilize lesser vessels.

The seven windows were now a dirty, hazy brown-green but I remembered seeing the "ice blink," an intensely white sky on the gray horizon telling of heavy pack ice ahead that would force us to struggle through to our destination; and I could see the "water sky," those dark patches on the low charcoal-white stratus clouds that told of leads toward open water and easier access to our goals. In barren landscapes of the polar south without clear navigational markers we relied on the skies and their stark atmospherics for guidance.

I could see back thirty five years and way beyond that—all the way back fifty years to the dawn of this adventure, when as a thirteen year old boy I came home from seventh grade every day for weeks and months hoping that there would be a letter from the nation's and world's foremost polar explorer.

I'd read all the books, devoured the *National Geographic* articles about his expeditions.

Written a letter.

And waited for a response. I had a hundred questions about a continent enshrouded in mystery, protected by terrible winds and numbing cold—"How did men survive the six months of dark winter? What lay beneath the two miles of ice? What was the continent's history?" and on and on and on.

I longed to sledge across the great ice shelves in the. tracks of this explorer, Rear Admiral Richard E. Byrd, to visit his famous outpost at the Bay of Whales, Little America, and to fly over the great mountain ranges like the Queen Maud Range that he had seen on his pioneering flights.

From one hundred feet above the murky Sacramento River on this blue sky morning I could see way back, as if peering through a telescope at the young universe in formation, gazing back to the big bang of our origins.

I saw back to the dawnings of two new eras: Byrd opened Antarctica to exploration by air in 1928, initiating what came to be the Navy's onslaughts on the coastlines only a few years later. Byrd pioneered the unmasking of the entire continent.

At the same time as the US and world economies came tumbling down, Edwin Hubble, peering through his 100 inch telescope at Mt. Wilson in California, confirmed that those barely visible fuzzy white specks on the face of the night sky were actually other galaxies, other worlds, outside and beyond our Milky Way, racing away from us at speeds initiated by the Big Bang some 14.5 billion years ago. Byrd and Hubble opened our worlds of exploration to the discovery of new universes, near and far. No longer could we consider our Milky Way the only island universe in the sky. Now we had billions of galaxies with hundreds of billions of stars each, all part of this incredibly expanding universe revealed to us today with the power and majesty of the Hubble Space Telescope. Byrd had written me in 1952 about the world's "shrinking with an ever increasing acceleration." But what neither Byrd nor Hubble imagined was that the expansion of the Universe is accelerating, *gaining* speed, all because of a very strange force known as "dark energy."[27]

And many of these discoveries in astronomy are enhanced by the little machine my father helped to develop in 1952, the computer. The same machine my mother worked on after midnight of her family's fortunes became evident.

The wonders never cease.

And now I could plainly see that my journey had commenced with a book, one book and its companions had changed an entire life.

It had led to a near worship of heroes of bright metal and bold stripe, men who dared to sledge beyond their limited horizons as Cherry-Garrard said, "for the sake of science." But I had learned along the way that some men are not what they seem. Wishful projection and yearning for companionship had turned the Little America of the pictures and stories into a fabled Xanadu or Shangri-La. It was neither. It was, in reality, a *little* America, full of the passions and power plays we all live with daily. Some men would wreck the whole endeavor for a daily swig of their blessed Golden Wedding Whiskey.

---

27 See Christopher J. Conselice 2007 "The Universe's Invisible Hand" *Scientific American*, Vol 296, No. 2 February, p. 34.

And standing here in Loft Conn where Byrd must have stood on his last voyage to Antarctica in 1956, I remembered that Byrd had planned Advance Base in 1934 as a three man outpost, but, according to Norman Vaughan, the Admiral decided he must go it alone. Vaughan, whom Byrd wanted as his second-in-command, figured out from Byrd's explanations that the Admiral wanted all the glory (as well as the considerable risk!) of this exploit for himself. He needed more publicity for this expedition since there was no dramatic polar flight as there was in 1929. That's when Vaughan declined to join the Second Byrd Antarctic Expedition—there would be no challenge for him. Vaughan was a man of bold stripe and integrity.[28]

One more deception, one more mask rent asunder like *Glacier's* busting up the thick pack ice. Byrd. . .Beaufort. . .sea-leopards rocketing through calm seas. . .and Antarctica herself. . .Unmasked, yielding to persistent inquiry.

But, in the end, this community survived the onslaughts of terrible hurricane force gales sweeping down from the polar plateau, because men realized they needed each other to survive. Antarctica held them together as men whose very lives depended upon companionship, a willingness to offer a shipmate your warm flesh in order to stave off the onset of frostbite. The cold, the crevasses and the danger lurking beneath the ice kept these men of bold stripe and daring alive.

It must also have been the fascination, recorded by Scott in 1903, with "the unknown" that kept men together. Antarctica set their imaginations ablaze with possibilities suggested by discovering a fossil fern embedded in shale rocks holding coal seams near the South Pole. Dr. Wilson must have imagined the South Pole and Beardmore Valley in a warmer climate where these ferns grew and where we now know dinosaur-like creatures also roamed. All alone out prospecting for clues to the mystery while his companions worried so intensely about their return to Cape Evans after "losing" the race to Amundsen.

The unknown for Antarctica now is not where she has been. But what is her fate? What will become of her blessed ice flows and polar ice caps if global warming continues, if we persist in pumping hot green house gases like carbon dioxide and chlorofluorocarbons into the atmosphere?

---

28 Norman Vaughan, 1990, *With Byrd at the Bottom of the World: The South Pole Expedition of 1928-1930*. Stackpole Books.

Little America led to McMurdo, to the two mile high plateaus of Vostok and to Erebus, that fuming volcano. But Little America also led to being an educator in New York City, where we discovered snow high up in the Catskills in June. It led to Project Adventure for young people who wanted to become teachers. Here we climbed walls, slid down zip lines and leapt off 50 foot high telephone poles into mid air to grasp the trapeze handle.

For almost two decades I had worked with undergraduates who wanted to become teachers. I had also been teaching my old favorites, *Crime and Punishment*, *A Portrait of the Artist as a Young Man* and *Black Boy* to literature students. Here we experimented with students' generating portions of the curriculum with their curiosities about Raskolnikov, Stephen Dedalus and Richard Wright. Their questions became the sum and substance of much of what we explored.

I had to experience the joys of probing the depths of students' thoughts and feelings about these strange, wondrous humans who struggled through life whether it be in pre-Soviet St. Petersburg, Russia or Dublin or our own Deep South. I wanted to expand our own humanity by imaginatively re-creating the characters in literature, not just with discussions, but through the film, poetry, pictures, and violin sonatas[29] all created and composed by students to share their understandings of these great adventures with me and their classmates. We spent as much time acting out the lives of Raskolnikov and Dmitri Karamazov as we did in intense debates. This was the joy of teaching, seeing young people grab a role and struggle with it toward personal meaning. Again, we were in Claire Slattery's class, imagining new roles, taking command.

Eventually I heard the call of Little America to form a cohort of educators who would explore new horizons. Like the adventurers from that frontier town, we needed to find authentic settings wherein the young people could learn the arduous task of teaching. We couldn't learn how to teach within the four walls of a university classroom. So we left the Spanish architecture of Montclair State University for Paramus, New Jersey, there to test ourselves

---

29 After reading *Othello*, I challenged the students in a literature class to find any artistic means to share with me and others the depth of their understandings about the play, its themes and major characters. Todd van Beveren wrote a sonata for viola based on themes in *Othello* that he performed in class and at his final music recital.

in the classrooms of elementary, middle and high school students. We needed to be explorers pressing beyond our own limited horizons, facing the realities found in any public school classroom—-kids who loved biology, art, math and literature and those who would rather play video games.

We drew on one of my more intense experiences—spending seven days sailing with Outward Bound in Penobscot Bay. During this week in Maine we camped out on Bay islands, rowed our wrists and forearms to a frazzle when there was no wind, rappelled down and up the granite quarries of Hurricane Island, balanced our way across wires suspended high above the pine tree tops, zapped down the "zip line" and spent lots of time building camaraderie and debriefing our challenges.

This is the kind of experience I wanted young teachers to have. Fortunately, Paramus High School had Project Adventure, a series of physical, social and emotional challenges involving low and high ropes elements, wall climbing and indoor elements like leaping for a brass ring. Project Adventure had built the facilities at Hurricane Island for Outward Bound and their motto was "Challenge by Choice."

Six times a year at Paramus we scrambled up wooden walls, had ourselves belayed as each of us attempted to climb up the sides of the school, leapt out of tall trees into mid air and swung down the zip line and climbed telephone poles all with the goal of creating teamwork, experiencing the risks of taking a chance, of failing and starting over.

On one particularly misty early May morning, Cheryl sat in her warm up suit outside the gym. We were scheduled to go out to the horizontal and vertical telephone poles and she was dressed for the role. She had had a spectacular semester in our college course where we asked Cheryl, Erika, Tina, Aldo, Carolyn and Betiana and all others to go into their classrooms, teach lessons that challenged students to think through complex problems or issues within the prescribed curriculum, be video-taped, view the tape with their mentor and then write up their own analyses of these experiences. Today was to be her third and final experience. Her mentor, Gary Pearl, had been most supportive of her. Whenever a student turned to him, sitting in the rear of the classroom, to ask a question, he motioned up to where Cheryl was working. "Ask Mrs. Wiest," he said constantly, giving her as much control as she wanted. She was at the conn.

That misty morning was to be her culminating classroom experience, bringing to bear all the strategies we had worked on in class, asking good, challenging questions, being able to follow up with quality responses that urged students to go deeper with their thinking, to search for answers and, finally, to reflect on what they had learned.

"I'm not going up there, Dr. Barell," Cheryl said. "It's raining and I've got my last teaching to do at ll this morning. I don't want to mess myself all up."

"OK," I said.

I walked out of the corridor and into the mists feeling saddened. I thought if anybody would try this—"Challenge by Choice" it would be Cheryl, but she's decided not to.

It's her choice. Period.

She's writing her own *Twenty Below* right now. Cheryl's at the helm where she needs to be, where all students need to be.

As I got closer to the telephone pole, Carolyn and Betiana said, "Cheryl's on her way out." I looked around, and saw her. That sight of Cheryl in her blue sweat suit nicely contrasting with her slightly blond hair made my morning.

Once again, I tried the leap from atop one of the telephone poles out about six or eight feet toward the suspended brass ring. We were about fifty feet above the ground. I balanced myself on one and a half feet trying to muster up the courage and the best take off.

I leapt into the air.

Missed.

Aldo tried it and grabbed the brass ring! He'd accepted the risk of slogging across those terrains full of crevasses and succeeded.

"Way to go, Aldo!" the cohort shouted from down below.

We were elated. No one in our cohorts had done that before. I asked him how he did it. "I don't know what I did special." The gym teacher, our mentor that year, Bill Whitney, had whispered something to him just before he climbed up. "What'd Bill say?" I asked.

"He said a girl had just done it yesterday."

Aha!

Then Cheryl took the challenge. She climbed up, slowly. The video camera, as always, was rolling so we had a record of all these doings, so we could see ourselves as others saw us. She got up onto the pole. "What am I doing up here!" she yelled to the green playing field below peopled with her friends. Cheryl daily drove about an hour and a half to get to Paramus. It would have been so much easier for her to just go to classes at Montclair. But she chose this field-based cohort program, "for the challenge," she said.

She leapt off into space. We held our breaths.

Cheryl missed the bar, but made everything else.

We debriefed. "What did you feel? What did you observe? What did you learn?"

"This whole Project Adventure is like a metaphor for teaching," said Tina. "It's just like going in there everyday—taking a risk, trying out different things."

Erika thought of herself as young Rocky Balboa ("I'm a tough guy now...") after climbing a tree and sliding down the Zip Line to the encouragement of her mates.

Cheryl went back to school, taught her last lesson. She'd done all of this before the full semester of student teaching. When September came around and she and Gary started working together full time, she took over two of his classes on the very first day. She was prepared. She'd accepted the challenge. "I always want the maximum experience, " she said. "I want to do everything I can to get the most out of it."

A year later, while she was out teaching full time at her first job, a national magazine for educators featured Cheryl on the cover with a short article about the cohort program.

"Go for it, Dr. Barell!" they had all yelled, Tina, Carolyn, Cheryl, Erika, Aldo, and Betiana. What was I doing standing on this telephone pole with barely enough room for one foot preparing to leap into the void, yes with ropes and safety lines held by Connie Story of Paramus?

On each of four separate attempts I missed, but Aldo Casal made it during the second cohort and so did Art Settembrino during the third and last company of young rebels. This was a height I never enjoyed.

Then why?

I did it because of Scott, Byrd and the others, because they still mattered in my life; because once upon a time there had been this community of intrepid explorers who dared to set out over the Ross Ice Shelf to delineate the contours of a continent. I was up on this telephone pole because of a passion for community, born at 23 Webster Park, born from the pages of *Little America* and extending forward for more than fifty years.

In the end these young teachers became ambassadors for adventure, for turning schools from repositories of glacial amounts of factual data into expeditions searching for knowledge out on the frontiers, where we each pose the questions that disturb the universe, questions that lead to fascinating discoveries.

One of these discoveries reported by Russian and other glaciologists concerns the highest point of the polar plateau, Vostok: that two miles beneath where I stood in 1964 lies a pristine fresh water lake the size of our Lake Ontario. The world's scientists are poised just a few kilometers above the surface of this pre-historic lake figuring out how to penetrate it without contamination. Researchers say, "Lake Vostok is absolutely devoid of interference. The youngest water in it is 400,000 years old. It doesn't know anything of human beings, fossil fuels, or plastics."

The amazements proliferate. . .

In the end Antarctica is more than a continent.

Shaped like a question mark Antarctica is our model of the inquisitive human spirit. She is

> Restless, constantly, yet glacially on the move. . .
>
> Mysterious and often enshrouded in darkness, ignorance and secrecy. . .
>
> At other times shining brilliantly in open blue sky, with clear pristine air undiluted by civilization and its overindulgences. . .
>
> Ultimately, she invites our deep and prolonged wonderings that probe beneath surface appearances for the rocks of reality beneath.

This has been the greatest of all adventures, growing up with parents and grandparents who set the dream on course, who fostered the spirit of wondering, who read the letters, who held out the expectations as irrelevant as they seemed—"Goals, Plan, Work"—for a young adventurer of thirteen.

And standing once again in Loft Conn, this confined fairly clean but very confining space where we once charged through the pack ice of pinks, greens, browns and subtle shades of blue, I think I understand how I came to "live" for this half century within my own little america.

Peering back to the dawn of this adventure I realize that it has been the story of America, both little—-the stories of so many 23 Webster Parks--and writ large—-of exploring the planet and outer space. America, the land of infinite possibilities for those with opportunity to seek them; America, the land that gives birth to a life force full of wondering, speculating, imagining, searching, pioneering, forever questioning and investigating, doubting, challenging assumptions. America—-where you can write, create and live out your own story. America, the land of fulfilled and unfilled promise for millions, especially for those who never quit and believe "There's no such word as CAN'T."

Little did Byrd realize the kinds of changes that are altering the delicate balance of life on this our blue dot in the darkness of space, nor could he have foreseen how our universe accelerates in its expansiveness. But were he able he would again climb up to 'Loft Conn and command this ship through the ice.

And this is what I've come to realize:

We all set our sights on receding horizons as we struggle toward our goals. On these life journeys we fall down into hidden crevasses; most of us struggle upwards to pull ourselves out and set our courses anew.

Byrd, my father and I are all more alike than different. Each had his visions of the future and each failed and succeeded in a multitude of different ways.

Standing here in 'Loft Conn I finally realized how Byrd has changed my life infinitely for good and how he is still a model of daring, courage, and supreme organizational ability. I know I could never have mounted an expedition to any continent at the young age of forty as he did.

I keep the chart he signed and his first letter, framed by Nancy Ann, over my desk together with a picture of *Glacier* with four Emperor penguins looking as if they just returned from McMurdo Sound full of krill ready to regurgitate, standing there in some awe of the haze gray behemoth churning her course toward Hut Point.

Was he "gold, pure, shining and unalloyed"? Yes, when I was thirteen. Now, that question doesn't matter.

Afterword: A View from the Conning Tower

Rear Admiral Richard E. Byrd remains a guiding spirit of my own adventures to this date, adventures that take me across the written page to envision stories not yet told, and fresh journeys with educators intent on setting the highest standards for inquiry and achievement.

When out in the cold on the streets of New York City, I remember his telling me on that day at 9 Brimmer Street with his very distinctive Virginia intonations, "I've been colder here in Boston than I ever was in Antarctica." I recall good Titus Oates of the Inniskilling Dragoons crawling out into the raging blizzards on the Ross Ice Barrier in 1912 never to be seen again. And I bundle up in my Land's End parka warmed by their memories of courage, men of very bold stripe.

I also recall Byrd's telling me at our first meeting of riding in a cab in his summer khaki uniform, seeing two men fighting on the sidewalk. He asked the driver to pull over, took off his cap and jacket and stepped out of the cab to arbitrate only to have the pugilists turn from each other to attack him.

"Imagine that, John?" he asked, again treating me as a member of his family.[30]

Our childhood heroes are always with us, serving as advisory admirals of the fleet, ready to suggest new course destinations for the ships we command.

We forge ahead and beyond the pressure ridges and crevasses that manacle our pathways, ever mindful of those tiny white specks that might blossom out on our faces in the fierce winds of progress. We hold the controls firmly yet gingerly in our own hands pressing toward new frontiers.

"All Ahead Full! Balls to the wall!"

Come, be an adventurer, a sailor over the seven seas in pursuit of your own south poles.

---

30 A recent article in the *Boston Globe* described 9 Brimmer Street as having been converted by Byrd's children to condominiums in 1982. "The building is now split into three apartments: the current owner is selling off the first and second floors where Byrd worked and he and his family entertained guests, as a condominium listed at $2,295,000." I met him in his study on the first floor and then we proceeded up the circular stairway to the second floor where we watched the film "Operation High Jump." Paul Sullivan "The Admiral's Quarters," 18 February, 2007.

About the Author

John Barell currently works with educators around the country who are interested in challenging their students to ask good questions, conduct purposeful investigations, think critically and reflect.

He resides in New York City with his wife, Nancy, and can be reached at jbarell@nyc.rr.com or through his website, www.morecuriousminds.com.

Current Blogs: http://morecuriousminds.blogspot.com (about education, art, science and current events)

And http://antarcticdreams.com (building upon *Quest* to fashion Life Lessons from the Southern Continent).